LEWIS AND CLARK

The Maps of Exploration 1507-1814

Portrait of Meriwether Lewis by Charles Willson Peale, ca. 1807.
Courtesy of Independence National Historical Park.

Portrait of William Clark by Charles Willson Peale, ca. 1807-08.
Courtesy of Independence National Historical Park.

LEWIS AND CLARK

The Maps of Exploration 1507-1814

Written by
Guy Meriwether Benson
with
William R. Irwin and Heather Moore Riser
with a Foreword by
John Logan Allen

University of Virginia Library

Published on the occasion of the exhibition
Lewis and Clark: The Maps of Exploration 1507-1814
University of Virginia Library
www.lib.virginia.edu/speccol/exhibits/lewis__clark

Designed by Carolyn Weary Brandt

Library of Congress Cataloging-in-Publication Data

University of Virginia. Library.
    Lewis and Clark : the maps of exploration, 1507-1814 : Univer-
sity of Virginia Library.
      p. cm.
    Includes bibliographical references and index.
    ISBN 1-57427-138-5 (hardcover : alk. paper)
    1. Cartography--United States--History--Exhibitions. 2. Carto-
graphy--West (U.S.)--History--Exhibitions. 3. West (U.S.)--Dis-
covery and exploration--Maps--Exhibitions. 4. Lewis and Clark
Expedition (1804-1806)   I. Title.
GA405.5.U54 2002
917.804'2'074755481--dc21

2002009725

ISBN 1-57427-138-5

Printed in Singapore

Published by Howell Press, Inc.
1713-2D Allied Lane
Charlottesville, VA 22903
(434) 977-4006
www.howellpress.com

CONTENTS

FOREWORD

Maps are the capstone of the landscapes of our imagination. Of the various graphic or visual means we have of representing landscapes, maps are the most enduring and persistent. They remain when nearly everything else in our visual imagery has been erased by the passage of time or buried under the accretions of new information. Unlike other art forms, maps carry the *imprimatur* of "science" and are assumed—usually mistakenly—to be constructed out of information that is at once more exact and objective than that contained in drawings, paintings, or even photographs. Almost no one assumes that the Hudson Valley looks exactly like it was portrayed by the early romanticists of the mid-nineteenth century or that the Grand Canyon is precisely depicted in the paintings of Thomas Moran. But maps—even those that contain obviously apocryphal information—are different: the images obtained from maps persist beyond the boundaries of time and, often, beyond the bounds of rational thought as well. Precisely for this reason, an exhibition of map imagery in the McGregor Room of the University of Virginia Library, showing the collective depictions of the American continent in general and the American West in particular over the centuries preceding the Lewis and Clark Expedition of 1804-1806, allows us to view the West as Lewis and Clark, and their sponsor Thomas Jefferson, would have viewed it on the eve of the transcontinental journey. As we look back on America's exploratory epic from the vantage point of the Lewis and Clark Bicentennial, the maps contained in *Lewis and Clark: The Maps of Exploration 1507-1814* open for us a view of the American West from the west portico of Monticello, a view that takes us beyond the Blue Ridge to the west, over the horizon of sight but not beyond the horizon of the mind.

Lewis and Clark: The Maps of Exploration 1507-1814 showcases maps that were either in the personal library of Thomas Jefferson or well known to him. As such, they may be fairly taken to represent the cartographic baseline for Jefferson's understanding of the broader dimensions of western geography. They reveal Jefferson's evolving conceptions of the finer points of the geography of the western interior: the idealized pyramidal height-of-land from which rivers flowed toward the cardinal compass points and the seas on all sides of the continent; the proximity of the headwaters of the Missouri and some stream flowing to the Sea of the South; the continental symmetry of western mountains being viewed as analogs of the Blue Ridge and Appalachians; and, above all, the absolute certainty that through the western interior there lay a viable Passage to the Pacific through which Jefferson and his young Republic could realize both their geopolitical and their commercial ambitions.

The maps in the first section are primarily European productions, the first maps to penetrate the mists of the Ocean Sea and expose the view of a New World to inquiring minds in the merchant counting houses of England and the Low Countries, the courts of France and Spain, the petty principalities and city states of Germania and the Italian peninsula. These maps are useful in delineating Jefferson's faith—and it was faith, accepted without the application of reason—in a Passage. Beginning with the great German cartographer Martin Waldseemüller's 1507 map depicting for the first time the two continents of the New World, down to the detailed North American map published 160 years later by Nicolas Sanson, founder of the Dieppe school of cartography in France, these maps all held out the promise of reaching the East by sailing west, a promise that motivated Thomas Jefferson,

Meriwether Lewis, and William Clark in 1803 no less than it had motivated Columbus in 1492.

The second and third sections contain maps of continental penetration by French and Anglo-American explorers, a cartography of achievement and hope that both recorded the consequences of westward venturings and limned a path for future exploration. From the maps of Louis Hennepin and Guillaume Delisle, the Baron Lahontan and Nicholas Bellin, Herman Moll and Daniel Coxe, the Loyal Company of Albemarle County, Virginia (which included among its members both Thomas Jefferson's father, Peter, and schoolmaster, the Reverend James Maury) derived the information on the pyramidal height-of-land and the theoretical geography of a symmetrical continent that focused attention on the Missouri River and "whatever river heading with it" as the logical path to the Pacific. From the charter of the Loyal Company to the maps drawn by some of its members, we find evidence of the importance of geographical thinking to a segment of the Virginia gentry into which Thomas Jefferson and Meriwether Lewis were born.

The fourth section contains the items that were the essential "tools of empire" of the Lewis and Clark Expedition. These include the maps used in the preparation and planning of the Lewis and Clark Expedition and those derived from the Expedition itself. Among these tools of empire, none stands out more than the map of the American West drawn by Nicholas King in 1803, following discussions on source maps (most of which are included in this catalog) among Jefferson, Lewis, and Albert Gallatin, Jefferson's Secretary of the Treasury and a key player in the planning process for the Lewis and Clark Expedition. The purpose of King's map was to crystallize, in one cartographic document, the information on the West and the Passage to the Pacific that was judged to be the best by Jefferson and his fellow participants in planning America's epic exploration.

On this great map we can see the American West as Thomas Jefferson saw it in 1803. There are mountains in the vicinity of the headwaters of the Missouri and Columbia. To the north are the mountains crossed by Alexander Mackenzie in 1793 on his way to the Pacific, mountains that had been appearing in British literature and on British maps for a century. To the south are the mountains long known as the "mountains of New Mexico" that had been described in French and Spanish accounts of Louisiana for at least as long a period of time. There was nothing in the literature that said the two ranges had to be connected but Jefferson's imaginary geography was based not just on the literature but also upon interpretations of it—and upon experience. Weaned on the principles of symmetrical geography and growing up at the base of the Blue Ridge, it is likely that Jefferson envisaged a highland region connecting the Stony Mountains of the north and the New Mexico mountains of the south. This highland region lay no great distance from the sea (as verified by exploration along the Pacific coast in the 1790s) and through it the upper Missouri and upper Columbia could be connected with a portage. This was the American Passage to the Pacific. When Meriwether Lewis took his leave from Jefferson in 1803 and headed west for a rendezvous with William Clark, the Nicholas King map and all it portrayed went with him. The implications of what followed were not just continental but global in scope.

John Logan Allen
The University of Wyoming

PREFACE

Since the original exhibition of Lewis and Clark maps was displayed in Alderman Library's McGregor Room in 1995, the exhibition web site has received more than 163,000 hits and library staff have shown the maps from the 1995 exhibition to nearly 700 scholars, map enthusiasts, and school children. As the numbers suggest, the story of Lewis and Clark's heroic expedition across the country remains perennially popular among history buffs and, as the 200th anniversary of the explorers' departure on the expedition approaches, the subject is steadily growing in popularity.

The 1995 exhibition, entitled "Exploring the West from Monticello: A Perspective in Maps from Columbus to Lewis and Clark," was the brainchild of Guy Benson, a member of the Lewis and Clark Trail Heritage Foundation. The Trail Heritage Foundation meets annually to celebrate the route that Lewis and Clark followed on their voyage of discovery. In the summer of 1995, the foundation met in Charlottesville to acknowledge Jefferson's hometown as the beginning of that trail. Mr. Benson wanted to create an exhibition that would display the maps that Jefferson had owned as he planned the Lewis and Clark expedition.

Happily, the McGregor Library in the Special Collections Department of the University of Virginia Library already had in its collection nearly all of the maps needed to tell the story of the planning of the expedition. The exhibition was very popular while it was on display from July to September 1995. But the real impact has lived on well beyond the physical exhibition. The University of Virginia Library published an accompanying catalog with the support of the Library Associates and with a grant from the Virginia Foundation for the Humanities. Nearly 2,000 copies of this catalog have been distributed. Also, after the physical exhibition came down, we created a web version of the exhibition using the exhibition text and photographs of the maps—a brand-new idea at the time.

Over the years, the catalog, the web site, and, indeed, the very subject of Lewis and Clark have remained so popular that, as the bicentennial approached, the Library wanted to be involved in the celebration. In 1999, University of Virginia President John Casteen appointed a committee of academics from around the University to commemorate the Lewis and Clark bicentennial. Plans for the celebration include speakers, colloquia, student involvement, and much more, representing an interdisciplinary initiative that has drawn together members from departments around the University as diverse as anthropology, architecture, environmental science, and history. The Library, for its part in the University celebration and commemoration of the expedition, is remounting the Lewis and Clark exhibition and republishing the catalog. The exhibition will be on display in the McGregor Room of the University of Virginia Library from November 2002 through May 2003.

Lewis and Clark: The Maps of Exploration 1507-1814 reflects a re-envisioning of the original catalog. We have omitted a section on navigational instruments that was in the original catalog, and we have added some new items that were received since the first exhibition. In 1995, when digital technology was in its infancy, we used black and white photographs of the maps in printing the catalog and creating the web site. We have now re-imaged all of the maps using state-of-the-art digital technology and have used these images both in this publication and on the newly designed web site www.lib.virginia.edu/speccol/exhibits/lewis__clark.

We would like to thank from the University of Virginia: Sara Lee Barnes, Lynda Fuller Clendenning, Bradley Daigle, Jeffrey L. Hantman, Alan B. Howard, Melissa Kennedy, Jenry Moorsman, Kathryn Morgan, Peter Onuf,

Hoke Perkins, Michael Plunkett, Mercedes Quintos, George Riser, Douglas Seefeldt, Clinton Sisson, and the University of Virginia Lewis and Clark Bicentennial Project.

Others we would like to thank: Peter A. Agelasto III; Richard E. Ailstock; Arlene Anns; Joan Benson; Nick Bon-Harper; Ralph Ehrenberg; Ronald E. Grim; John R. Herbert; Kat Imhoff; Lloyd T. Smith, Jr.; Lewis and Clark Trail Heritage Foundation; Independence National Historical Park, National Park Service, Philadelphia, Pennsylvania; Geography and Map Division, Library of Congress, Washington, D.C.; and Beinecke Rare Book and Manuscript Library, Yale University, New Haven, Connecticut.

Heather Moore Riser
Special Collections
University of Virginia Library

INTRODUCTION

No one knew more about the geography of North America in his own day than Thomas Jefferson. A skilled surveyor and cartographer, he was engaged in a lifelong search for geographic knowledge. Jefferson studied the history of geography from the emerging worldviews of the ancients to the latest exploratory charts and maps of the American West. He amassed a remarkably thorough and varied collection of explorers' accounts, geographic works, and maps for his personal library. Moreover, although Jefferson himself never traveled west of Warm Springs, Virginia, he was America's first great Westerner. Promoter of four attempts to reach the Pacific, he personally planned the successful expedition led by Meriwether Lewis and William Clark from 1804 to 1806.

Lithograph of Thomas Jefferson by P.S. Duval after Gilbert Stuart. (Special Collections, University of Virginia Library)

Thomas Jefferson's intellectual curiosity drew him into an accelerating, three-hundred-year-old quest to find a water route to Asia. To understand Jefferson's views of the West and the nature of the quest to the Pacific, the University of Virginia Library and the Lewis and Clark Trail Heritage Foundation have put together an exhibition and book of maps and journals. *Lewis and Clark: The Maps of Exploration 1507-1814* examines the planning of the Lewis and Clark Expedition and the cartographic tradition that made the expedition possible. The exhibition shows the evolving views of the American continent and the "Passage to the Indies" as they appear in maps up to the Lewis and Clark Expedition. It focuses especially on the earliest cartographic representations of America and the Northwest Passage, the results of early expeditions to the Mississippi basin in search of a route to the Pacific Ocean, and the early exploration of the Pacific Northwest.

The idea of traveling west to reach the East tantalized humankind ever since the discovery that the earth was round. European geographers of the late fifteenth century—the first generation of men capable of verifying the theories of the ancients—envisioned a great western ocean and a few mythical islands between Europe and Asia. Most of these men knew that the distance to the nearest point in Asia—believed to be Cipangu (the island of Japan)—was beyond the reach of the sailing ships of their day. However, ongoing debate over the true distance to the Orient encouraged Christopher Columbus in his belief that it was only 2,400 miles to Cipangu. After being rebuffed by many European courts, Columbus persuaded the sovereigns of Spain to sponsor his voyage across the Atlantic Ocean in 1492. When he spotted land only three months into his journey, Columbus felt vindicated that the fringes of Asia were closer to Europe than others had maintained. To his dying day, Columbus thought he had reached some part of Asia.

Following Columbus's initial exploration, many other voyages of discovery brought news of the lands to the west. For a generation after Columbus's first sighting of the New World, cartographers continued to show the new discoveries as islands between Europe and Asia. Martin Waldseemüller in 1507 was one of the first to show these "islands" in continental proportions. As the image of new American continents to the west took hold, this contribution to geographical knowledge seemingly precluded a direct seafaring route to Asia. Nonetheless, geographers and explorers expected to find either a water route through or around the new landmasses or a short land passage over them to the Indies. The maps in section I, covering a period from just after Columbus to 1650, reflect these possibilities and also show the emerging shape of the North American continent.

The maps in section II examine the French contributions to cartographic knowledge of North America as they pursued their quest to find a passage to Asia. In the ninety years from the expedition of Jacques Marquette and Louis Joliet until the fall of Quebec in 1759, the French explored the Great Lakes, much of the area from the Appalachian Mountains to the Rocky Mountains, and the region between the Mississippi River and the Spanish settlements in New Mexico. They also pushed westward in Canada to within sight of the Rockies. For French explorers, the Missouri River emerged as the most likely route to the Pacific Ocean. In their efforts to explain the topography of North America, the French developed two new geographical theories: pyramidal height-of-land and symmetrical geography (see page 27).

While sections I and II show the early maps of America from a European perspective, section III, "Albemarle Adventurers," explores the contributions made to western exploration by the Virginia gentry that included the families of Thomas Jefferson and Meriwether Lewis. Fifty years before Lewis and Clark set off on their expedition, a group of Albemarle County residents who were personally and intellectually related to Thomas Jefferson and Meriwether Lewis planned an expedition to the West via the Missouri River.

Section IV presents the maps used in the planning of the Lewis and Clark Expedition. The items reveal the state of cartographic knowledge of the West up to the time Meriwether Lewis set off from Pittsburgh in 1803. This section also chronicles the explorations that inspired the Lewis and Clark Expedition and the further refinement of geographic theories of North America. An 1810 manuscript map by William Clark and the journals of the expedition—the two-volume *History of the Expedition under the Command of Captains Lewis and Clark*—indicate the results of the expedition.

I.

Novus Orbis:
Images of the New World, 1507-1669

This section shows the evolution of geographic views of North America from the first maps to represent the New World as continents to the beginning of French exploration in the Mississippi Valley. When Europeans learned of the immense new continents that blocked their way to Asia, they did not abandon hope of finding a direct passage to the Orient. In 1507, Martin Waldseemüller (c. 1470-1518) produced the very first map depicting the New World as two continents and the first to designate the Southern landmass "America," after Amerigo Vespucci. This map, only one copy of which survives, shows a strait separating two narrow continents and emptying into a compressed Pacific Ocean. The sea lying to the north of the northern continent suggests an open passage from Europe to Asia. Explorers and geographers confronted the possibility that the new landmasses could be bypassed altogether, passed through via straits, or traversed on short overland routes.

Waldseemüller's map and accompanying book, *Cosmographiae Introductio* (St. Dié, 1507), were widely copied and very influential. Vasco Núñez de Balboa found such a land route in Central America when he crossed the isthmus of Panama to the "Southern Sea" in 1513. In 1524 Giovanni da Verrazano, a Florentine employed by the king of France to find a passage to the Pacific Ocean, mistook the large body of water to the west of the Outer Banks of North Carolina for the Pacific Ocean. The map by Sebastian Münster (page 15) shows this false "Sea of Verrazano." Nearly a century later, John Farrer's 1652 map of Virginia, which located the Pacific

Ocean just over the Blue Ridge, confirmed the persistence of this yearning to find an easy route to Asia (page 23).

By the 1600s, the hope for a Panama-like isthmus crossing in North America faded. Moreover, once the Spanish gained control of the southern sea routes, French and English efforts to reach Asia shifted northward in the quest to find a "Northwest Passage." Several generations of seamen—including Jacques Cartier, Martin Frobisher, Henry Hudson, Samuel de Champlain, and others—searched for this route across the continent. Although these

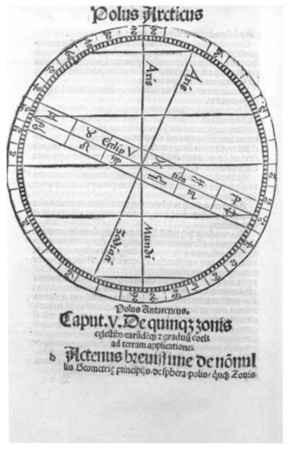

Illustration from Waldseemüller's Cosmographiae *(Strasbourg, 1509). (The Tracy W. McGregor Library of American History, Special Collections, University of Virginia Library)*

explorers made several discoveries of "passages" that were later proven false or nonviable, their efforts added the St. Lawrence River, the Great Lakes, and the Hudson Bay to the maps of North America. All of the maps in this section show some form of Northwest Passage. The quest to find this route persisted until Captain James Cook finally disproved the existence of the Northwest Passage in 1778.

At the dawn of the sixteenth century, the leading centers of European cartography were in Italy and Germany. Cartographic expertise soon shifted, however, first to the Low Countries, and then to France. The rival exploring nations Portugal and Spain treated their new geographic discoveries as state secrets and protected those secrets under penalty of death. Nevertheless, some geographic information was smuggled out of Spain and still more was obtained from maps seized from captured Spanish galleons. Around 1540 several Spaniards, including Fray Marcos de Niza, Francisco Vásquez de Coronado, and Juan Rodríquez Cabrillo, explored the interior of the present-day United States and the coast of California. Spanish place-names such as "Cibola," "Quivira," and "Sierra Nevada" began appearing on maps of America by the 1560s. One example is the 1570 map of Abraham Ortelius (page 17).

Despite growing European knowledge about the New World, a considerable number of aberrations on the maps of the late sixteenth century reveal the limitations of geographic knowledge in this period. The Sea of Verrazano and the Northwest Passage proved to be two New World geographical fantasies. Other erroneous representations long influenced explorers and mapmakers. A map by Cornelius Wytfliet (page 19) places "Quivira" on the Northwest coast instead of in the middle of the continent. Similarly, Nicolas Sanson's map (page 25) depicts California as an island and shows the "Rio Del Norte" (Rio Grande) emptying into the Gulf of California.

In the mid-1500s, Gerhard Mercator developed his famous projections that significantly improved cartographic science. Mercator's approach, as refined by Edward Wright, is examined on pages 20-21.

Sebastian Münster.

"[Die Nüw Welt] Tavola dell' isole nuove."

From *Cosmographia universale.* Cologne, 1575.

Sebastian Münster (1489-1552) was a German mathematician, cartographer, professor of Hebrew, and, for a time, monk. He was the first mapmaker to produce separate maps of the four known continents and the first to publish a separate map of England.

This woodcut map is a version of the first map to show North and South America connected to each other but separate from any other land mass. The map, "Novae Insulae, XVII Nova Tabula" was originally published in Münster's edition of Ptolemy's *Geographia* (Basel, 1540) and in Münster's masterwork, *Cosmographia*, in 1544.

Cosmographia was one of the most influential works on geography in the mid-sixteenth century; it was translated into five languages and published in forty different editions. Münster's map was the most widely circulated New World map of its time. It depicts the false Sea of Verrazano and the Northwest Passage and presents a view of North America that precedes the Spanish explorations to the interior of the continent.

The Münster map shown here, from an Italian edition of *Cosmographia* published in Cologne in 1575, differs from the version in Ptolemy's 1540 *Geographia* only in its title and labeling.

(Special Collections, University of Virginia Library)

Abraham Ortelius.

"Americae sive Novi Orbis, Nova Descriptio."
In *Theatrum Orbis Terrarum*. Antwerp, 1570.

Abraham Ortelius or Ortel (1527-1598), a rare book dealer in Antwerp, produced a map of the world in 1564. Ortelius's world map is especially noteworthy because it incorporates information from Jacques Cartier's explorations of 1534-1541 and shows the St. Lawrence River as a gateway to the Pacific Ocean. Although he is generally considered more of a compiler and publisher of maps and atlases than a cartographer, Ortelius traveled with Gerhard Mercator and ranks second only to Mercator among Flemish cartographers.

Inspired by his friend Mercator and borrowing from him, Ortelius compiled a book of maps coordinated in size and content. This book, *Theatrum Orbis Terrarum* (Antwerp, 1570), with maps engraved by Franz Hogenberg, is considered the first modern atlas.

The map shown here is from the second edition of the atlas, printed in the same year as the first edition. Between 1570 and 1612, Ortelius's atlas appeared in forty-two editions and seven languages. One remarkable feature of this book is that at a time when cartographers copied from the work of others without attribution, Ortelius scrupulously credited ninety-one sources.

"Americae sive Novi Orbis" provides a reasonably accurate outline of North America and improves upon the representation of the St. Lawrence River from Ortelius's earlier world map. The map from the atlas shows a very narrow Pacific Ocean, however, and it situates New Guinea due south of California. "Americae sive Novi Orbis" also locates "Quivira" too far to the west. Here Ortelius seems to have relied on Francisco López de Gómara's popular *Historia general de las Indias* (1552). Gómara mentions that Coronado located the wealthy kingdom of Quivira at 40 degrees latitude. Since Coronado also re-ported that he had reached the sea, cartographers interpreted this to mean that Quivira must be near the West coast.

Ortelius's "Americae sive Novi Orbis" also shows "Anian" in the Northwest. Anian was a mythical kingdom mentioned in Marco Polo's travel accounts. Before it appeared in America on this map, Anian was generally believed to be located off the northern coast of Asia; curiously, Ortelius's world map published just six years earlier locates Anian on the Asian mainland.

Compared to other contemporary maps, "Americae sive Novi Orbis" provides much more detail of the New World. Ortelius was also one of the first cartographers outside of Spain to adopt the nomenclature designated by the Spaniards Niza, Coronado, and Cabrillo on their American explorations.

(The Tracy W. McGregor Library of American History, Special Collections, University of Virginia Library)

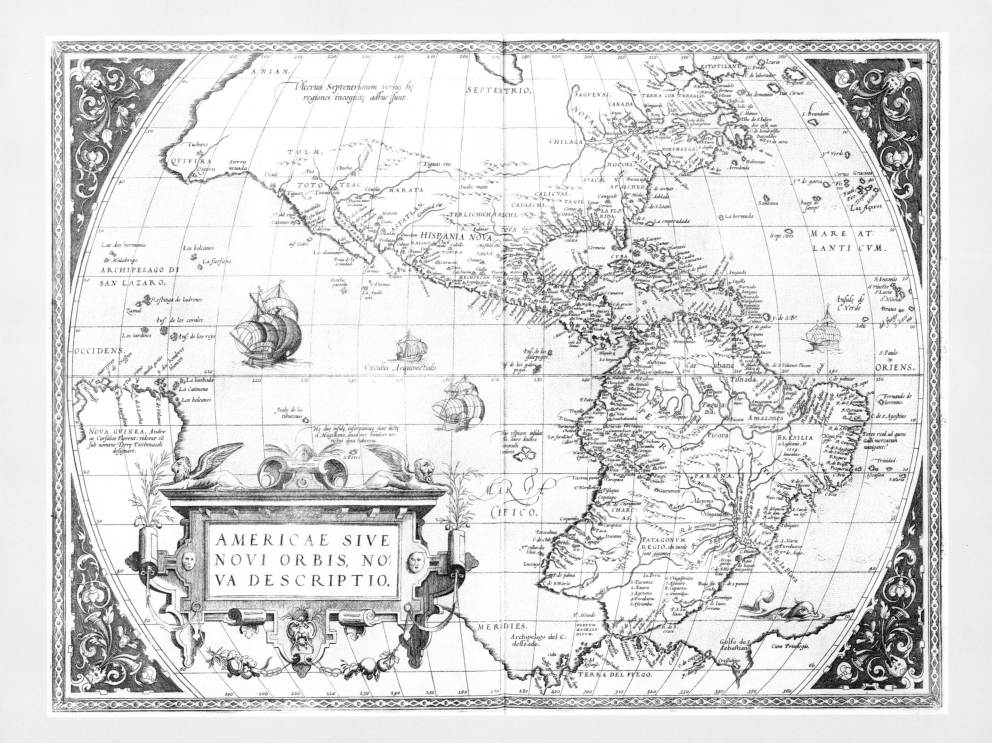

AMERICAE SIVE NOVI ORBIS, NOVA DESCRIPTIO.

Cornelius Wytfliet.

"Granata Nova et California."

and

"Limes Occidentis Quivira et Anian."

In *Descriptionis Ptolemaicae augmentum.* Louvain, 1597.

Cornelius Wytfliet was a Flemish cartographer. His atlas *Descriptionis Ptolemaicae augmentum*, published in Louvain, Belgium, in 1597 as a supplement to Ptolemy's *Geographia*, was the first atlas devoted exclusively to the New World. The atlas contains nineteen regional maps of the Americas, including the two listed above. It also provides information on the discovery of the New World and on the geography and natural history of North and South America.

The Albert and Shirley Small Special Collections Library owns three copies of the Wytfliet atlas: a second edition in the Paul Mellon Collection and 1598 and 1603 editions in the Tracy W. McGregor Library. The two maps shown here depict the West coast of North America. In "Granata Nova et California," the coast of upper California runs almost due west until it reaches Cape Mendocino ("C. Medocino"). Wytfliet represents "Septem civitatem Patria"—the legendary Seven Cities of Cibola that inspired Francisco Vásquez de Coronado's gold-seeking expedition of 1540-1542—as a cluster of cities around a lake that is connected to the Gulf of California by a river. The map designates Cibola ("Ceuola") as a separate city. On the other map, "Limes Occidentis Quivira et Anian, 1597," "Quivira" appears too far to the west. Finally, like many other maps of the period, a world map (not shown) in Wytfliet's atlas depicts the Straits of Anian connecting to the fabled Northwest Passage from the Atlantic Ocean.

(The Paul Mellon Collection, Special Collections, University of Virginia Library)

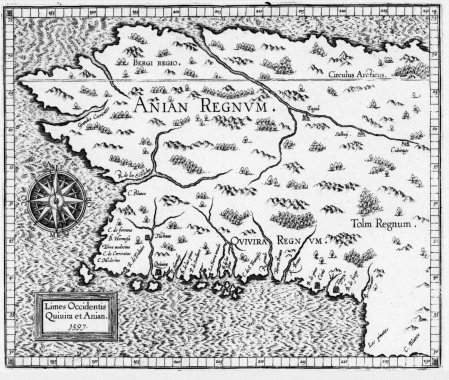

Edward Wright.

"A Chart of the World on Mercator's Projection." c.1599.

In *The Principall Navigations, Voiages, Traffiques and Discoveries of the English Nation*, compiled by Richard Hakluyt. London, 1598-1600.

The great geographer and mathematician Gerhard Mercator (1512-1594) revolutionized cartography when he developed an isogonic cylindrical projection that mapped a sphere onto a flat plane. Mercator expected that his projection would be a valuable tool for navigators, although he neglected to provide practical guidelines on how use it. Edward Wright (1558?-1615), a professor of mathematics at Cambridge University, modified Mercator's system and published his results in *Certaine errors in Navigation* (London, 1599) and in a later, improved edition entitled *Certaine errors in Navigation, detected and corrected* (London, 1610). Wright's book contained new mathematical tables and instructions on plotting straight-line courses on maps based on the Mercator projection. The system developed by Wright contributed to the supremacy of the British Navy and is still in use today.

Wright published "A Chart of the World on Mercator's Projection" in 1600 based on his projection of a globe engraved by the English globe maker Emery Molyneux in 1592. This was the first map to use Wright's improvements on Mercator's projection. The map, sometimes designated the "Wright-Molyneux Map," was also published in *The Principall Navigations, Voiages, Traffiques and Discoveries of the English Nation* (London, 1598-1600), compiled by Richard Hakluyt. Considered a sixteenth-century cartographic landmark, the Wright-Molyneux Map is alluded to in Shakespeare's *Twelfth Night*, when Maria says teasingly of Malvolio: *"He does smile his face into more lynes, than is in the new Mappe, with the augmentation of the Indies."*

Unlike many contemporary maps and charts that represented the often-fantastic speculations of their makers, Wright's "Chart of the World" offers a minimum of detail and even leaves areas blank wherever geographic information was lacking. These undefined areas are especially evident along Wright's coastlines. For example, the coast of California above Cape Mendocino is blank.

Wright's world map depicts a wider Pacific Ocean than other maps of its time. On the American continent, Wright labels upper California "Nova Albion," adopting the name Sir Francis Drake gave to the region; other maps designated this area "Anian." "Quivira" still appears on the West coast. Further to the east, the map also shows a "Lake of Tadouac" reminiscent of the Sea of Verrazano. This lake is connected to the Atlantic Ocean by a river that appears to run south of the St. Lawrence River; it is also connected to a large body of water to the north. Lake Tadouac is apparently an early reference to either the Hudson Bay or to the Great Lakes, neither of which were "discovered" by Europeans until eleven or twelve years after Wright's map was published. Wright's map is also one of the earliest maps to use the name "Virginia."

(The Tracy W. McGregor Library of American History, Special Collections, University of Virginia Library)

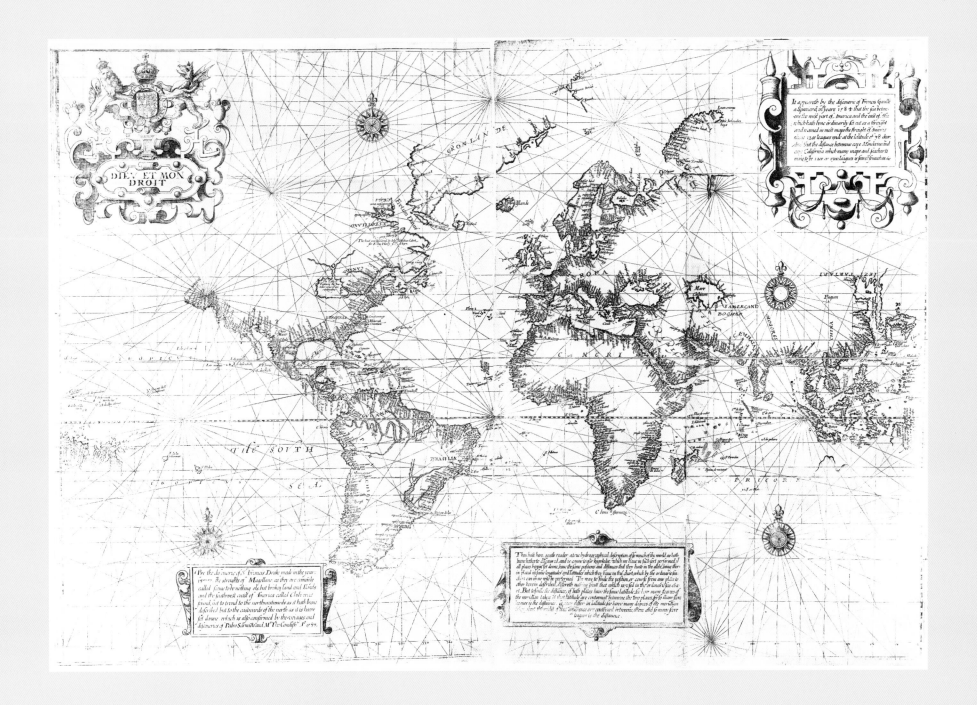

John Farrer.

"A mapp of Virginia discovered to ye Hills." 1651.

John Farrer or Ferrar (1590-1657) was born in London. He was a member of the Royal Council of the Virginia Company and deputy treasurer of the company from 1619 to 1622. An active investor in and promoter of the colony, he supported the establishment of the silkworm industry in Virginia. Farrer wrote a description of the Virginia colony in *A Perfect Description of Virginia* (London, 1649); Edward Williams incorporated this description into *Virgo Triumphans: or, Virginia richly and truly valued*, first published in 1650. Farrer also named his daughter after the colony "so that speaking unto her, looking upon her, or hearing others call her by name, he might think upon both at once." Virginia Farrer (1620-1688) continued her father's efforts to introduce silk culture into Virginia and was the compiler of the later versions of her father's map.

In his personal copy of Williams's *Virgo Triumphans*, Farrer wrote in the margin: "But a map had binn very proper to this Book For all men love to see the country as well as to heare of it." That copy, now owned by the New York Public Library, contains a rough manuscript map drawn in Farrer's hand and entitled: "A mapp of Virginia discovered to ye Falls." An engraved version of this map first appeared in the third edition (1651) of *Virgo Triumphans*.

Farrer's map depicts an astonishingly narrow North American continent in which the Pacific Ocean appears just beyond the Appalachian Mountains! Farrer attributed his representation of the continent to the English mathematician and cartographer Henry Briggs. Briggs, who was the first mapmaker to show California as an island, may have conflated the mountains that lay to the east of California with the mountains that lay to the west of Virginia. A belief in the false Sea of Verrazano could also have led Farrer to the conclusion that the American continent was extremely narrow. In *A Perfect Description of Virginia*, Farrer writes:

> from the head of James River above the falls . . . will be found like rivers issuing into a south sea or a west sea, on the other side of those hills, as there is on this side, where they run from west down to the east sea after a course of one hundred and fifty miles.

Farrer's map legend also notes that a ten-day march westward from the head of the James River will bring the traveler to rivers that run into the "Indian Seas."

Another remarkable feature of the Farrer map is the Northwest Passage, which is formed by a river to the north that connects the Hudson River to the "Sea of China and the Indies." Farrer's map labels many place-names in Virginia and Maryland for the first time. It also provides details on the Swedish and Dutch settlements north of Virginia.

The map shown here is a fourth state (c.1652) in which *Falls* in the title is changed to read *Hills*. In this version of the map a narrow isthmus blocks the Northwest Passage. Virginia Farrer compiled this version of the map.

(The Tracy W. McGregor Library of American History, Special Collections, University of Virginia Library)

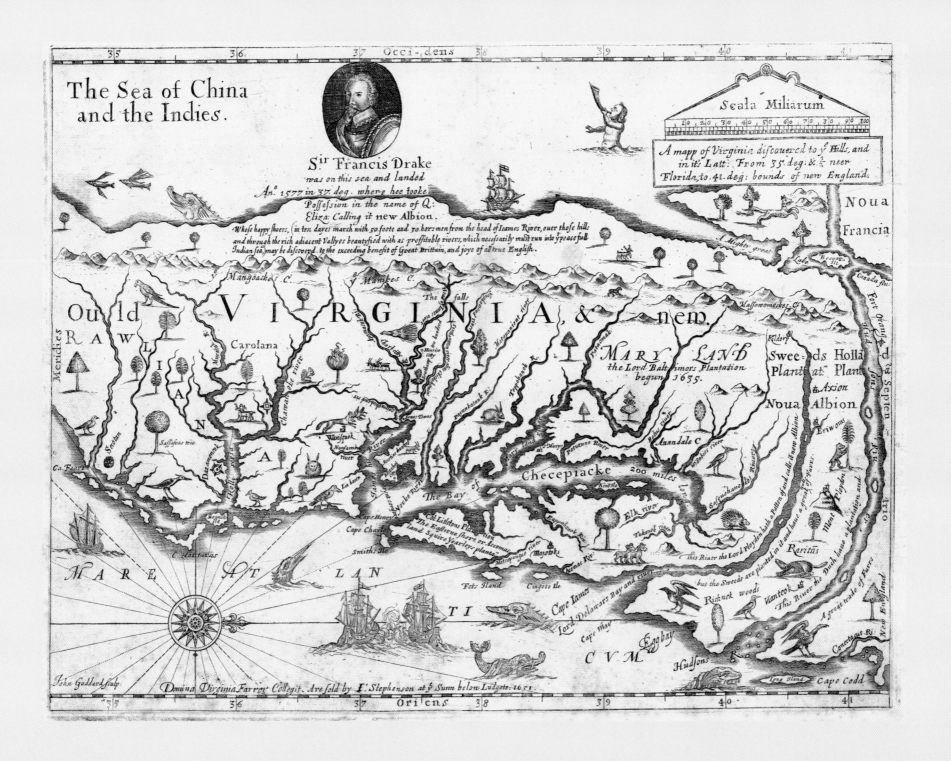

Nicolas Sanson.

"Amérique Septentrionale." 1669.

Nicolas Sanson (1600-1667) was the outstanding French cartographer of the mid- to late-seventeenth century and is considered the founder of the French school of cartography. His involvement with maps began when he drew maps and illustrations for his own historical books. His career coincided with a period of bold French exploration and expansion. As the French were building up their store of geographic knowledge and skills, Sanson's work came to the attention of Louis XIII. Much impressed, Louis became Sanson's patron and appointed him Geographer to the King around 1630. Due largely to the Sanson family's map-publishing business, the patronage of Louis XIII and Louis XIV, and the work of the newly-formed Académie royale des sciences, the seat of cartography shifted from the Low Countries to France in the latter part of the seventeenth century.

"Amérique Septentrionale" was first published in 1650 and revised in 1656 and 1669. It appeared in atlases in 1658 and 1667. The French used this map as well as Sanson's "Le Canada ou Nouvelle France, etc." (1656) in their explorations of the interior of North America. "Amérique Septentrionale" is the first map to show all five Great Lakes. A ring of mountains surrounding the southeastern portion of North America limits the length of the Mississippi River, but the map suggests the possibility of a Northwest Passage. It is the first map to label Santa Fe ("S. Fe"), and it locates "Quivira" to the east of New Mexico for the first time. It also depicts the "R. del Norte," or the Rio Grande, originating in a lake and emptying into the Gulf of California.

The most notable feature of "Amérique Septentrionale" is its representation of California as an island. Sixteenth-century maps had typically shown lower California as a peninsula. In 1620, however, the Dutch found a chart, drawn about 1602 by Father Antoine Ascension, showing California as an island. This chart, along with written reports from Ascension and the Spanish explorer Juan de Oñate, led Henry Briggs and many other cartographers to represent California as an island. California continued to appear as an island on maps of America even after the explorations of Father Eusebio Francisco Kino proved otherwise around 1700 (for example, see pages 36-37). Finally, in 1747, King Ferdinand of Spain issued a royal decree that California was not an island!

The 1669 version of "Amérique Septentrionale" shown here differs from Sanson's original 1650 map in its detail of the Gulf of California and labeling of oceans.

(Special Collections, University of Virginia Library)

AMERIQUE
SEPTENTRIONALE

Par N. Sanson Geographe Ord.re du Roy.

*Revene et changée en plusieurs endroits
suivant les Memoires les plus recents*

Par G. Sanson Geogr.e Ordinaire du Roy.

A PARIS

*Chez Pierre Mariette rue S. Iacques a l'Esperãce
Avec privilege de sa Ma.te pour 20 ans.*

OCEAN SEPTENTRIONAL

Cercle du Pole Arctique

ISLANDE I.

M E R
D E
N O R T

MER DE CANADA ou NOUVELLE FRANCE

NOUVELLE FRANCE

TERRES ARCTIQUES

GROENLANDE

VIEIL GROENLANDE

Premier Meridien

ISLES BRITANNIQUES

ISLES AÇORES

TERRE DE LABORADOR ou NADA ou NOUVELLE BRETAGNE

M. GLACILLE

CANADA

NOUVEAU MEXIQUE

APACHES DE NAVAIO

APACHES DE XILA

APACHES VAQUEROS

ISLE DE CALIFORNIE ou MER VERMEIO

MER VERMEIO ou MER ROUGE

NOUVELLE GRANADE

QUIVIRA

FLORIDE

MER DE NORT

Cercle Tropique du Cancer

MEXIQUE ou NOUVELLE ESPAGNE

ISLES ANTILLES

ISLES CARIBES

GOLFE DE MEXIQUE

MER DES ISLES

OCEAN ATLANTIQUE

M E R
D E
S U D

Occident

Septentrion

Midy

Orient

AMERIQUE MERIDIONALE

II.

An Easy Communication
Betwixt the River Meschacebe, and the South Sea

The French followed the Portuguese, Spanish, and English to the New World. By 1504 French fishermen were harvesting the waters of the Grand Banks off Nova Scotia and Newfoundland. Soon contact with the Indians of the region led to a lucrative fur trade and a keener sense of American geography. Explorations by Jacques Cartier in the 1530s and 1540s and by Samuel de Champlain in the early 1600s pushed the fur trade inland up the St. Lawrence River. By 1650 the French had reached all five of the Great Lakes.

As the French expanded their Indian trade westward from the St. Lawrence, they continued the search for a water route to the Orient. Reports from western Indians of "Great Waters" even further to the west raised the French hopes of finding this passage. Although the Spaniards Hernando de Soto and Alvar Núñez Cabeza de Vaca were the first Europeans to see the Mississippi River during their expeditions to the interior of North America in the mid-1500s, more than a century passed before any other Europeans explored the Missouri or Mississippi rivers beyond the southwestern portion of the Mississippi basin.

French *coureurs de bois*, or trappers, were undoubtedly the first Europeans to reach the northern Mississippi. French explorers came within a three-day trip of reaching the Mississippi River in 1640 and may have reached it in 1659. Finally, in 1673, Jacques Marquette, a Jesuit missionary, and Louis Joliet, a fur trader, not only reached the Mississippi but descended it as far as the Arkansas River. Noting the large volume of water entering the Mississippi from the mouth of the Missouri River, which he called the "Pekitanoui," Father Marquette speculated that this river came from a great distance. The Indians told him that if he ascended the Missouri for five or six days and made an easy portage, he would reach another river that led southwest to a lake and joined another waterway that led to the sea. Marquette proclaimed: "I have hardly any doubt that it is the Vermillion Sea [Gulf of California], and I do not despair of discovering it someday." Alas, Marquette died two years later in 1675, before he could attempt this voyage.

In 1682 René Robert Cavelier, sieur de La Salle, descended the Mississippi and proved that the river emptied into the Gulf of Mexico as Marquette had also predicted. La Salle claimed the Mississippi River and all lands drained by the river and its tributaries for France, naming the territory *Louisiane* in honor of Louis XIV. Several members of La Salle's expedition noted the powerful current of the Missouri River. Father Louis Hennepin said that the Missouri could be ascended "for ten or twelve days to a mountain where they [the tributaries] have their source; and that beyond this mountain is the sea, where great ships are seen."

Over the next forty years French explorers, traders, miners, and missionaries explored the upper Mississippi, Ohio, Red, and Arkansas rivers and, most importantly, the Missouri River. The French had made contact with the Osage Indians and perhaps the Kansa Indians by 1700. In 1713 Étienne Venyard, sieur de Bourgmont, conducted a detailed survey while venturing up the Missouri River to the Platte River, but for more than seventy years, no one ventured further up the Missouri than Bourgmont.

Meanwhile, French exploration continued to the south. The French reached the Rio Grande in 1713 and Santa Fe in 1739. They built Fort Cavagnolle in 1744, near present-day Fort Leavenworth, Kansas, as a trading post and gateway to New Mexico.

Beyond this southernmost exploration, other French adventurers pushed westward along a more northerly route from Canada and the Great Lakes. Pierre Gaultier de Varennes, sieur de la Vérendrye, and his sons set off from Canada in the 1730s in quest of a route to the western sea. In 1739 they reached the Mandan Indian villages near the Great Bend of the Missouri (in present-day North Dakota). Two of Vérendrye's sons explored the area southwest of the Mandan villages. Indeed, by the time the French period in North America came to an end with the fall of Quebec in 1763 and the cession of Louisiana to the Spanish in 1764, the French had explored most of the territory that lay between the Appalachian Mountains and the Rocky Mountains in present-day Canada and the United States.

In addition to their legacy of extensive explorations, the French developed two geographical theories that were to play an important role in later cartographic representations of western North America. The *pyramidal height-of-land* theory postulated that America's great rivers all originated from centralized mountain heights before they dispersed to outlets in the Mississippi River, Hudson Bay, or Pacific Ocean. The French believed the sources of the rivers to be so close together that a short portage between them might be possible.

The second geographical theory, known as *symmetrical geography*, held that the topography of the western half of the continent was a mirror image of the continent's eastern landforms and waterways. Thus the drainage patterns of the rivers on the Pacific slopes of the western mountains would resemble those of the rivers on the eastern side of the Appalachian Mountains.

Further, once the construction of an eastern canal from the Potomac River to a tributary of the Ohio River appeared feasible, proponents of symmetrical geography believed that a similar internal improvement linking the rivers on the Pacific side of the continent might also be possible. A half-century later, one of the principal objectives of the Lewis and Clark Expedition was to resolve these geographical conjectures.

Knowledge of the French explorations spread quickly among those most interested in American geography. Cartographers produced maps based on information gleaned from the field journals and letters of adventurers and explorers such as Bourgmont, Vérendrye, and Champlain. Although many of these journals, letters, and maps were published, on the whole, this material was not widely distributed. Word of the French geographic discoveries spread far more quickly upon the publication of immensely popular "pulp" journals. Sensationalized accounts by Hennepin, Baron de Lahontan, Daniel Coxe, Pierre de Charlevoix, Robert Rogers, and Jonathan Carver contained a mix of firsthand investigations, information borrowed from other legitimate sources, and outright fictions. Often promotional in nature, these journals extolled the western lands and touted the ease of reaching the Pacific Ocean.

Thomas Jefferson was well aware of the French adventures in the West and the letters and journals generated from the French expeditions. Both the legitimate and the exaggerated accounts helped form Jefferson's image of the West and spurred his romantic hope of finding a water route to the Pacific Ocean.

Louis Hennepin.

"Carte de la Nouvelle France et de la Louisiane
  Nouvellement découverte."
In *Description de la Louisiane, nouvellement découverte
  au Sud'Ouest de la Nouvelle France*. Paris, 1683.

When Belgian-born friar Louis Hennepin (b.1640) entered the Catholic Church, he was assigned to the coast of France, where he heard tales from sailors returning from America that roused his passion for adventure. In 1675 he went to New France as a Recollect Missionary (an order of Reformed Franciscans). Father Hennepin was the historian on La Salle's first expedition in 1678 and produced the first written description of Niagara Falls. Sent by La Salle in 1680 to find the source of the Mississippi, he discovered the Falls of St. Anthony (he named them after his patron saint) at the present-day site of Minneapolis. Upon returning to France, Hennepin published *Description de la Louisiane* (Paris, 1683) along with an accompanying map, "Carte de la Nouvelle France et de la Louisiane Nouvellement découverte." The place-name "La Louisiane" appears for the first time on this map.

When Hennepin moved to Holland in the late 1690s he published *Nouvelle découverte d'un très grand pays situé, dans l'Amérique entre le Nouveau Mexique et la mer Glaciale* (Utrecht, 1697) and *Nouveau voyage d'un pais plus grand que l'Europe* (Utrecht, 1698). The former appeared in English in 1698 as *A New Discovery of a Vast Country in America* (London, 1698) and contained "A Map of a Large Country Newly Discovered." Since Hennepin was now free from the prohibitions of the French king, he offered a new account of his explorations in which he claimed to be the first European to descend the Mississippi River. His accounts were sometimes fanciful and inaccurate and his claim of discovering the mouth of the Mississippi was refuted by Andrew Ellicott and others. Nonetheless, his works were widely read and quite influential in shaping views of North America. Thomas Jefferson owned first editions of all three of Hennepin's books and consulted them in preparing his western treatise *An Account of Louisiana*, which he presented to Congress in November of 1803.

(The Tracy W. McGregor Library of American History, Special Collections, University of Virginia Library)

Louis Hennepin.

"A Map of a Large Country Newly Discovered in the
    Northern America situated between New Mexico and
    the Frozen Sea."
In *A New Discovery of a Vast Country in America.*
    London, 1698.

Father Hennepin popularized the notion of an easy communication or convenient passage from the Missouri River system to waters flowing into the Pacific Ocean. "A Map of a Large Country Newly Discovered" locates the mouth of the Mississippi River ("Meschasipi") too far to the west. The source of the Missouri River ("Otenta R.") appears as a lake in the mountains and is close to the source of the Rio Grande ("River of Magdalen"). His map from the 1697 French edition (not shown) depicts another river originating close to the source of the Missouri; this Great River of the West is shown flowing into the Gulf of California. By locating the origin of these great rivers in close proximity in the mountains, Hennepin's maps affirm the pyramidal height-of-land theory that dominated the geographic concepts of North America in the eighteenth century and influenced the planning of the Lewis and Clark Expedition.

*(The Tracy W. McGregor Library of American History, Special Collections,
University of Virginia Library)*

French Leagues
25 50 75 100 125 150
English Miles
75 150 225 300 375 450

HUDSONS BAY   Brador

NEW

FRANCE or CANADA

The upper Lake

Lake Huron or Karegnondi

Lake of the Illinois

Lake Erie or of the Cat

Great Villages of the Iroquois

VIRGINIA

NEW NETHERLANDS

FLORIDA

NEW MEXICO

PART OF NEW SPAIN

GULFE OF MEXICO

A MAP
of a Large Country
Newly Discovered
in the
NORTHERN AMERICA
Situated between
NEW MEXICO
And the Frozen Sea
together with the Course
of the Great River
MESCHASIPI
Dedicated to his Majy
WILLIAM III
King of Great Britain
By Father
LEWIS HENNEPIN
Missionary Recollect and
Apostolic Notary

Louis-Armand de Lom d'Arce, baron de Lahontan.

"A Map of ye Long River."
In *New Voyages to North-America,* London, 1703.

Louis-Armand de Lom d'Arce, baron de Lahontan (1666-1715?), was the son of a prominent civil engineer in the court of Louis XIV. In the 1680s Lahontan went to Canada with the Bourbon Regiment, where he served as Lord Lieutenant of the French colony at Placentia in Newfoundland. He commanded Fort St. Joseph (in present-day southwestern Michigan) in 1687 and explored the Great Lakes before returning to the East coast. Baron de Lahontan claimed to have traveled to the northern portions of the Mississippi River and to the villages of the Osage Indians on the Missouri River, but it was his journey to the Long River on his trip back from Fort St. Joseph that captivated the attention of adventurers who dreamed of finding a passage to the Pacific.

According to Lahontan, during a four-month journey in the winter of 1688-1689 his party of three hundred men explored the Long River or, as it is labeled on his map, the "Rivière Morte" or "Rivière Longue." The expedition traveled up the Long River about 800 miles from the Mississippi. At this point Indians told him that he was about 450 miles from a great salt lake located near some high mountains. Lahontan insisted that the Indians had shown him a deerskin map that depicted a large river running to the western sea. His own map suggests this passage to the Pacific Ocean.

Nouveaux Voyages de Mr. le baron de Lahontan, dans l'Amérique Septentrionale chronicles Lahontan's journey on the Long River as well as his travels throughout New France from 1683 to 1694. This book, which included his original map of the Long River, was published in 1703 at The Hague in two- and three- volume French editions and in London in a two-volume English edition, *New Voyages to North-America.* Lahontan also issued a separate account of his conversation with an Indian, *Dialogues de Monsieur le baron de Lahontan et d'un Sauvage, dans l'Amerique* (Amsterdam, 1704). Lahontan's widely published works were extremely popular in Europe. His depiction of the Long River appeared on the maps of other cartographers as late as 1785.

Thomas Jefferson owned the second English edition of *New Voyages to North-America* (London, 1735). Despite the fact that Lahontan's book was widely discredited by the second half of the eighteenth century, Jefferson deemed it an important work. He recommended it for inclusion in a national library in 1783 and later included it on a list of books relating to American travel that he called "a useful species of reading for an American youth."

(The Tracy W. McGregor Library of American History, Special Collections, University of Virginia Library)

The Dwelling Houses of the TAHUGLAUK, wich are 80 paces in length, according to the Draught that y̆ Mozeemlek slaves gave me upon y̆ Barks of Trees.

The Vessels us'd by the TAHUGLAUK in wich 200 men may row: provided they are such as som of y̆ Mozeemlek people drew to me upon y̆ Barks of Trees.

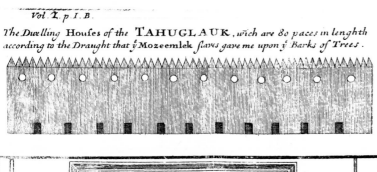

According to my computation such a Vessel must be 130 foot long from the prow to the stern.

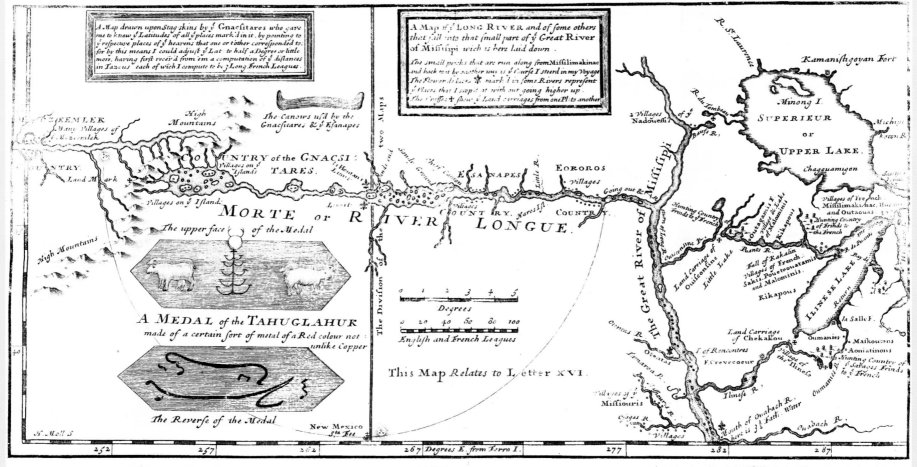

A Map drawn upon Stag skins by y̆ Gnacsitares who gave me to know y̆ Latitudes of all y̆ places mark'd in it, by pointing to y̆ respective places of y̆ heavens that one or other corresponded to. for by this means I could adjust y̆ Lat: to half a Degree or little more, having first receiv'd from 'em a computation of y̆ distances in Tazcus each of wich I compute to be 3 Long French Leagues.

A Map of y̆ LONG RIVER and of some others that fall into that small part of y̆ Great River of Missisipi wich is here laid down.

The small pricks that are run along from Missilimakinac and back to it broather way is y̆ Course I steerd in my Voyage. The Flower de luces ✹ mark'd in some Rivers represent y̆ places that I stopd at with out going higher up. The Crosses ✚ show y̆ Land carriages from one Pl: ts another.

The Division of the two Maps

The Canows us'd by the Gnacsitares & y̆ Esanapes.

MOZEEMLEK — Many Villages of y̆ Mozeemlek

High Mountains

COUNTRY of the GNACSITARES

Villages on y̆ Island

...COUNTRY

Land Mark

High Mountains

Villages on y̆ Island

MORTE or RIVER LONGUE

The upper face of the Medal

A MEDAL of the TAHUGLAHUK made of a certain sort of metal of a Red colour not unlike Copper

The Reverse of the Medal

New Mexico 5 th See

H. Moll S.

ESANAPES COUNTRY

EOROROS Villages

Little R.

Going out & R

R. St. Laurence

Kamanistagoyan Fort

2 Villages of y̆ Nadouessi

R. du Tombeau

Beuss R.

Minong I.

SUPERIEUR or UPPER LAKE

Chagouamigon

Villages of French Missilimakinac, Hurons and Outaouas

Hunting Country of Frinds to y̆ French

Ouisconsinc R.

Hunting Country Frinds to y̆ French

Puants R.

Outagamis & Villages of Malomini

Fall of Kakalin

Villages of French Sakis, Pouetouatami, and Malominis

Kikapous

Land Carriage of Ouisconsinc to Little Lake

ILLISE SE LAKE

la Salle F.

Oitanas R.

Land Carriage of Chekakou

Olonas R.

Temarca R.

T of Rencontres

F. Crevecoeur

Oumanies

Maskousins

Aoniatinons

Hunting Country of y̆ Savages Frinds to y̆ French

Village of the Illinois

Illinese R.

Villages of y̆ Missouris

Oates R.

Missouris R.

Mouth of Ouabach R. here is 3½ fath: Water

Villages

Ouabach R.

The Great River of Missisipi

Degrees
0 1 2 3 4 5

0 20 40 50 80 100
English and French Leagues

This Map Relates to Letter XVI.

252   257   262   267 Degrees E. from Ferro I.   277   282   287

Guillaume Delisle.

"Carte de la Louisiane et du Cours du Mississipi." 1718.

Claude Delisle (1644-1720) and his four sons replaced the Sansons as the preeminent family in the French school of cartography at the beginning of the eighteenth century. The most accomplished cartographer in the Delisle family was the child prodigy Guillaume Delisle (1675-1726), who became a member of the Académie royale des sciences at age twenty-seven and earned an appointment under Louis XIV as *géographe du roi* or royal geographer. He studied mathematics and astronomy at the Paris Observatory under Jean-Dominique Cassini, an Italian astronomer who devised the triangulation method of surveying and a new method for determining longitude based on the moons of Jupiter. Owing to his ability to plot continental outlines and drastically reduce the errors in determining lines of longitude, Guillaume Delisle is considered the first modern scientific cartographer.

In 1718 Guillaume Delisle published "Carte de la Louisiane et du Cours du Mississipi" which was based on "Carte de Mexique et de la Floride" and "Carte du Canada ou de la Nouvelle France," both credited to him in 1703, but actually made by his father, Claude. The 1703 maps incorporated geographic findings from the explorations of Marquette, Joliet, La Salle, Pierre le Sueur, and others. They depict the Missouri River extending as far as the country of the Omaha Indians, the "Rivière Longue" of Lahontan, the full course of the Mississippi River, and, for the first time, an accurate representation of the mouth of the Mississippi River and its delta.

The 1718 map shows an improved "Missouri R.," which Guillaume Delisle also labels "R. de Pekitanoni," after Marquette's name for the river. This map, however, does not include the excellent detail of the lower Missouri shown in another untitled Delisle map of 1718 based on the 1714 ex-plorations of Étienne Venyard, sieur de Bourgmont. Nonetheless, "Carte de la Louisiane et du Cours du Mississipi" incorporates other information from Bourgmont and also from Father Jakob Le Maire and Sieur Vermale. Delisle's map represents a tributary of the Missouri very close to the course of the Rio Grande ("Rio del Norte"). An extension of the upper Missouri, labeled "Riv. Large," runs to the west and around the northern edge of a chain of mountains. This "Riv. Large" may have been based on Lahontan's mythic Long River.

Delisle depicts a "Chemin des Voyageurs," or trading route, from the Mississippi River to the lands of the Omaha Indians near the Missouri River. "Carte de la Louisiane" is the first printed map to show the route of Hernando de Soto in 1539-1540; in addition, it traces the routes of other exploration between the Mississippi and the Rio Grande in the late 1600s and early 1700s. This is also the first map to refer to a variant of the name Texas ("Mission de los Teijas").

Delisle's "Carte de la Louisiane et du Cours du Mississipi" became the primary reference source for the lower Mississippi and lower Missouri river valleys and was used by other cartographers as late as 1797. This map is believed to be the oldest map consulted in the planning of the Lewis and Clark Expedition.

(The Tracy W. McGregor Library of American History, Special Collections, University of Virginia Library)

CARTE DE LA LOUISIANE ET DU COURS DU MISSISSIPI Dressée sur un grand nombre de Memoires entre autre sur ceux de M. le Maire Par Guill.me Delisle del Academie R.le des Scien.ce

Herman Moll.

"Map of North America to ye Newest and most Exact observations." 1720.

Herman Moll (d.1732) was born in the Netherlands and moved to London around 1680. He began his career as an engraver and earned renown as the foremost map publisher in England in the early eighteenth century. Moll was one of the first mapmakers to use London as the prime meridian for longitude. British authorities used his "Map of North America" and his 1715 "A New and Exact Map of the Dominions of the King of Great Britain on ye Continent of North America" (or "Beaver Map") to counter French claims to territory in North America. Throughout his career he published many maps of high quality covering all parts of the world.

The "Map of North America" shown here is one of the last maps to depict California as an island. Moll claimed that he knew of seamen who had sailed around the island. Moll, who had engraved the maps in Baron de Lahontan's *Nouveaux Voyages de Mr. le baron de Lahontan, dans l'Amérique Septentrionale* (The Hague, 1703), represents Lahontan's "Morte or R. Longue" as a northern tributary of the Mississippi flowing due west to a large lake in the mountains. On the other side of the mountains he shows a river running westward toward, but not reaching, the Pacific Ocean. The "Straits of Annian" also appear well to the north of California.

(The Tracy W. McGregor Library of American History, Special Collections, University of Virginia Library)

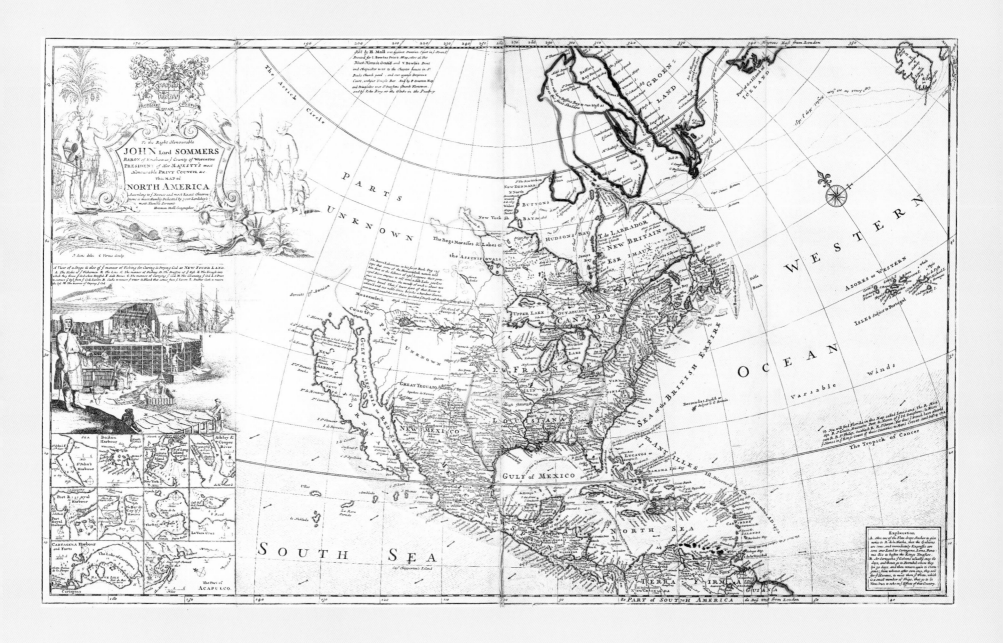

Daniel Coxe.

"A Map of Carolana and of the River Meschacebe."
In *A Description of the English Province of Carolana, by the Spaniards call'd Florida, And by the French La Louisiane.*
London, 1722.

Daniel Coxe (1673-1739) was the eldest son of Dr. Daniel Coxe of London, who received an immense land grant in the lower Mississippi valley from King Charles II. Daniel Coxe lived in the American colonies from 1702 to 1716. After returning to England he published an account of his travels and a description of the territory encompassed by his father's claim.

The map shown here appeared in the promotional tract *A Description of the English Province of Carolana, by the Spaniards call'd Florida, and by the French La Louisiane*, published in London in 1722 and republished in 1741. A legend on the map claims that "Carolana" is bounded to the west by New Mexico and to the east by "Prickt Lines from Port Royal in Carolina to the Palachean Mountains, & thence to the Lake Champlain." The Coxe map is the first map of the Mississippi valley done in English. An insert map, "A Map of the Mouth of the River Meschacebe," gives a fairly accurate representation of the Mississippi delta. The details on this insert map may have come from an expedition to the Mississippi commissioned by Dr. Daniel Coxe in 1698.

"A Map of Carolana and of the River Meschacebe" improved on earlier maps by eliminating the mountains along the Mississippi River and by accurately positioning the Ozark and Appalachian mountains. Certain fanciful features of American geography, such as a shortened "Long River" and a very large "Lake of Thoyago" in New Mexico, however, still appear on Coxe's map.

Although "A Map of Carolana and of the River Meschacebe" is not considered a cartographic landmark, *A Description of the English Province of Carolana* exerted considerable influence on geographical thinking about western North America by popularizing the concept of symmetrical geography. Coxe believed that the Mississippi valley demonstrated symmetrical geography and that the western slopes of what would be called the Rocky Mountains likewise mimicked the eastern slopes of the Appalachian Mountains. More important for the quest to find a passage to the western sea, Coxe promoted the notion of "an easy Communication betwixt the river Meschacebe [Mississippi River], and the South Sea."

The "easy communication" foretold by Daniel Coxe helped convince a group of Albemarle County land speculators known as the Loyal Company to plan an expedition to the West in the 1750s (see section III). Joshua Fry of the Loyal Company and Thomas Jefferson each owned a copy of Daniel Coxe's book, possibly the 1741 edition.

(The Tracy W. McGregor Library of American History, Special Collections, University of Virginia Library)

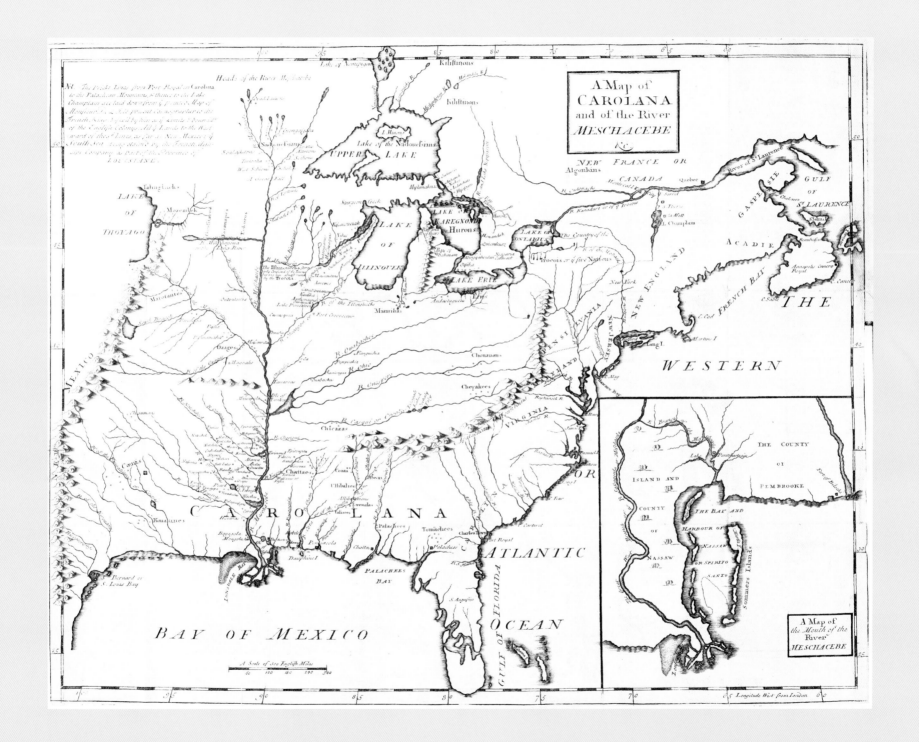

A Map of
CAROLANA
and of the River
MESCHACEBE
&c.

A Map of
the Mouth of the
River
MESCHACEBE

BAY OF MEXICO

CAROLANA

ATLANTIC OCEAN

WESTERN

THE

NEW FRANCE OR
CANADA

GULF OF
ST. LAURENCE

ACADIE

GULF OF FLORIDA

A Scale of 300 English Miles

Pierre François-Xavier de Charlevoix.

"A Map of the British Dominions in North America as
Settled by the late Treaty of Peace 1763."
In *A Voyage to North-America*. Dublin, 1766.

In 1720 the Duke of Orleans sent the Jesuit scholar and explorer Pierre François-Xavier de Charlevoix (1682-1761) to America to record events in New France and Louisiana and determine the best route to the Pacific Ocean. Charlevoix gathered geographic information from fur traders in Quebec before leading a voyage that took him up the St. Lawrence, through the Great Lakes, and down the Mississippi River to the Gulf of Mexico. In 1723 he recommended two strategies to reach the Pacific: one by ascending the Missouri, the other by establishing a mission among the Assiniboine Indians along the present-day U.S.-Canadian border and then pushing westward from that base. Charlevoix preferred the first route, but the French government backed the second. After surviving a shipwreck in the Gulf of Mexico, Charlevoix returned to France, where he published his views on North America in *Histoire et description générale de la Nouvelle France* (Paris, 1744).

"A Map of the British Dominions" is included in *A Voyage to North-America*, published posthumously in Dublin in 1766. The map offers an Anglo-centric view of North America. Note how the English colonial possessions of North Carolina and Virginia extend across the Mississippi River. Charlevoix also named four apocryphal islands in Lake Superior in honor of his patron.

Charlevoix promoted the pyramidal height-of-land theory and hypothesized that the Mississippi, Missouri, and Minnesota rivers originated in close proximity to each other. He believed that a traveler starting at the source of the Missouri River could easily reach, possibly by wagon, another river that ran to the Western Sea. Charlevoix estimated that the Western Sea was about 2,100 miles as the crow flies from the Sioux Nation. He described the junction of the Missouri and Mississippi rivers as "the finest Confluence in the World." Although he judged the two rivers to be equal in width, Charlevoix concluded, "the Missouri is by far the most rapid, and seems to enter the Mississippi like a conqueror."

Thomas Jefferson owned a copy of Charlevoix's *Histoire et description générale* (1744) and recommended it, along with the accounts of Hennepin and Lahontan, as a "particularly useful species of reading." He referred to Charlevoix's book as he developed his own ideas on Louisiana and the Northwest. *Histoire et description générale* contains "Carte de l'Amérique Septentrionale," a map of North America by Jacques Nicolas Bellin (page 47). The Bellin map represents Charlevoix's belief that a series of lakes and rivers connected Lake Superior to the Pacific Ocean.

(The Tracy W. McGregor Library of American History, Special Collections, University of Virginia Library)

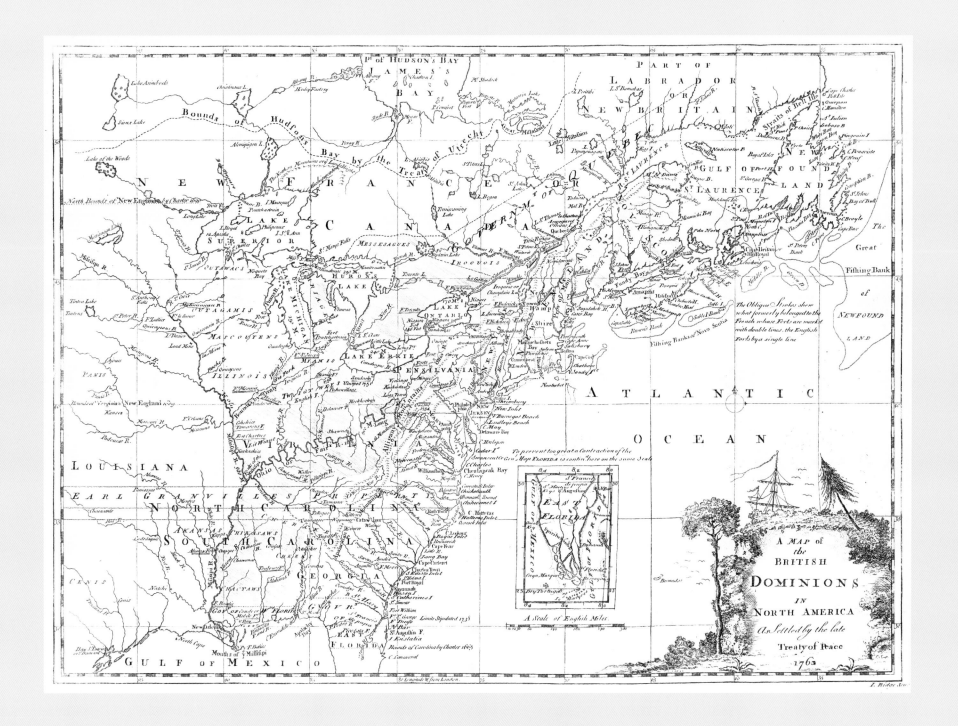

A MAP of the BRITISH DOMINIONS IN NORTH AMERICA As Settled by the late Treaty of Peace 1763

Jean-Baptiste Bourguignon d'Anville.

"Amérique Septentrionale." 1746.

Jean-Baptiste Bourguignon d'Anville (1697-1782), a French scholar and geographer, engraved his first map at age fifteen. He carried on the French school of cartography developed by the Sanson and the Delisle families and enjoyed a reputation as the finest mapmaker of his time. Although he apparently never left the city of Paris, he had access to the reports and maps of French explorers, traders, and missionaries. During his long career he accumulated a large collection of cartographic materials. D'Anville was particularly interested in Asia and produced the first reasonably accurate map of China in 1735.

D'Anville's American maps draw on material gathered from several French expeditions made during the first half of the eighteenth century, when the French were intent on preempting Spanish expansion into the Mississippi River valley and finding trade routes to the western Indians and Santa Fe. Around 1720, Jean-Baptiste Bénard de La Harpe undertook two expeditions to explore the Red and Arkansas rivers and part of what is now Oklahoma. At roughly the same time, Claude-Charles du Tisné journeyed by land to the source of the Osage River and explored southeastern Kansas. D'Anville engraved maps that incorporated the discoveries of La Harpe and Tisné and significantly improved the geographic knowledge of the Mississippi and Missouri river regions.

"Amérique Septentrionale" depicts a "Grande Rivière" running to the west out of the "Lac des Bois" with a note that it was discovered by an Indian named Ochagac, or Ochagach, a reference to the accounts of Vérendrye and his sons. The map shows the upper Missouri labeled as the "Pekitanoui R." Only the upper half of "Amérique Septentrionale" is shown here.

(The Tracy W. McGregor Library of American History, Special Collections, University of Virginia Library)

AMÉRIQUE
SEPTENTRIONALE
PUBLIÉE SOUS LES AUSPICES
DE MONSEIGNEUR LE DUC D'ORLEANS
PREMIER PRINCE DU SANG.

PAR LE Sr. D'ANVILLE

Jean-Baptiste Bourguignon d'Anville.

"Carte de la Louisiane." 1732.

In addition to "Amérique Septentrionale" (page 43), Jean-Baptiste Bourguigon D'Anville also engraved a map entitled "Carte de la Louisiane" in 1732. This map provides an accurate rendition of the lower Mississippi, the Arkansas, the Red, the Osage, and the lower Missouri rivers. Thomas Jefferson purchased seven maps by d'Anville in 1787. Although the titles of the maps he acquired are not known, Jefferson was familiar with d'Anville's maps of North America, including "Carte de la Louisiane." In a letter to Secretary of the Treasury Albert Gallatin regarding a newly commissioned map of North America, Jefferson discussed the use of d'Anville as a reference for the lower Mississippi basin. Jefferson may not have owned "Carte de la Louisiane," however, since Meriwether Lewis tried to obtain a copy of it in Philadelphia shortly before starting out on the Lewis and Clark Expedition.

(The Tracy W. McGregor Library of American History, Special Collections, University of Virginia Library)

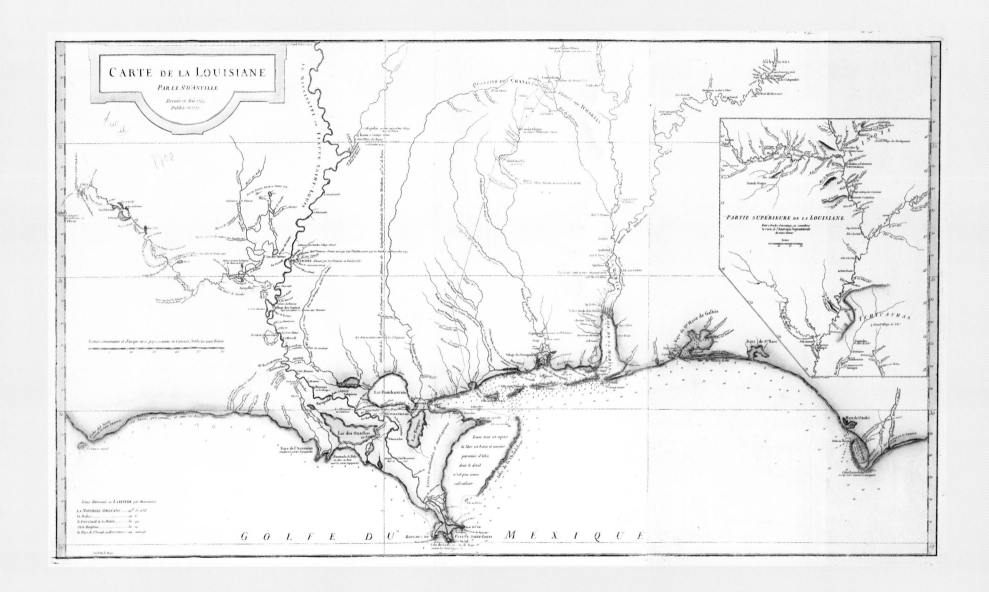

CARTE DE LA LOUISIANE

PAR LE Sʳ D'ANVILLE

Dressée en Mai 1732.
Publiée en 1752.

PARTIE SUPÉRIEURE DE LA LOUISIANE.
Pour s'étendre d'un ouvrage, on considère
la Carte de l'Amérique Septentrionale
du même Auteur.

GOLFE DU MEXIQUE

Jacques Nicolas Bellin.

"Carte de l'Amérique Septentrionale Depuis 28 Degré de
   Latitude jusqu'au 72." 1755.

Beginning in 1731, the French government sent Canadian-born Pierre Gaultier de Varennes, sieur de la Vérendrye (1685-1749), on several expeditions into western Canada to find a route to the Pacific Ocean. In 1739 Vérendrye reached the Mandan villages on the upper Missouri (though he did not recognize it as the Missouri). That same year his son, François, explored the Saskatchewan River. François and another son, Louis, later explored the area southwest of the Mandan villages to the Rocky Mountains.

Vérendrye and his sons relied extensively on information obtained from maps made by the Cree and Assiniboine Indians. Like other explorers, however, they misinterpreted much of what they transcribed from the Indian maps. Vérendrye came to believe that a River of the West connected with an opening on the Pacific coast discovered by Martin d'Aguilar in 1603. He also believed an inland sea called *La Mer de l'Ouest* was a receptacle for the River of the West. Both the River of the West and La Mer de l'Ouest turned out to be fictions, however. Likewise, Vérendrye perpetrated a myth of a Mountain of Bright Stone, or *Montagne de Pierre Brilliante*, when he misconstrued information he received from western Indians. Later, designations of the singular Mountain of Bright Stone evolved into the Shining Mountains, as the Rocky Mountains were called for many years.

Maps and charts from Vérendrye's expeditions were deposited at the Dépôt des Cartes et Plans de la Marine in Paris—the main depository of documents relating to French exploration in North America. Jacques Nicolas Bellin (1703-1772) served as the senior hydrographic engineer at the Dépôt. In addition to conducting seacoast surveys in France and throughout the world, Bellin made several maps of North America.

Bellin incorporated Vérendrye's findings, including the "Montagne de Pierre Brilliante," in the maps he made for Charlevoix's *Histoire et description générale de la Nouvelle France* (1744) and in the map shown here. At several points on "Carte de l'Amérique Septentrionale" (1755) Bellin acknowledges the lack of geographical certitude about western North America. In a note near the "Riv. des Assiniboile," Bellin indicates that this river might flow into "La Mer de l'Ouest." Likewise, he suggests a possible connection between "La Mer de l'Ouest" and two openings to the Pacific Ocean: the "Entrée de Juan de Fuca 1592" or the "Entrée des Martin d'Aguilar en 1603." He depicts the "Riv. des Mantons" as a separate river and in another note indicates that it may be connected to the lower Missouri. Finally, the lower section of Bellin's map borrows from maps by Guillaume Delisle and d'Anville, although Bellin locates the source of the Rio Grande further south than Delisle. On the Bellin map, the mountains of New Mexico form a southern range that is separated from the northern mountains by a gap.

The Bellin map was the basis for many later maps, including the map in Jonathan Carver's journal (page 67).

(Special Collections, University of Virginia Library)

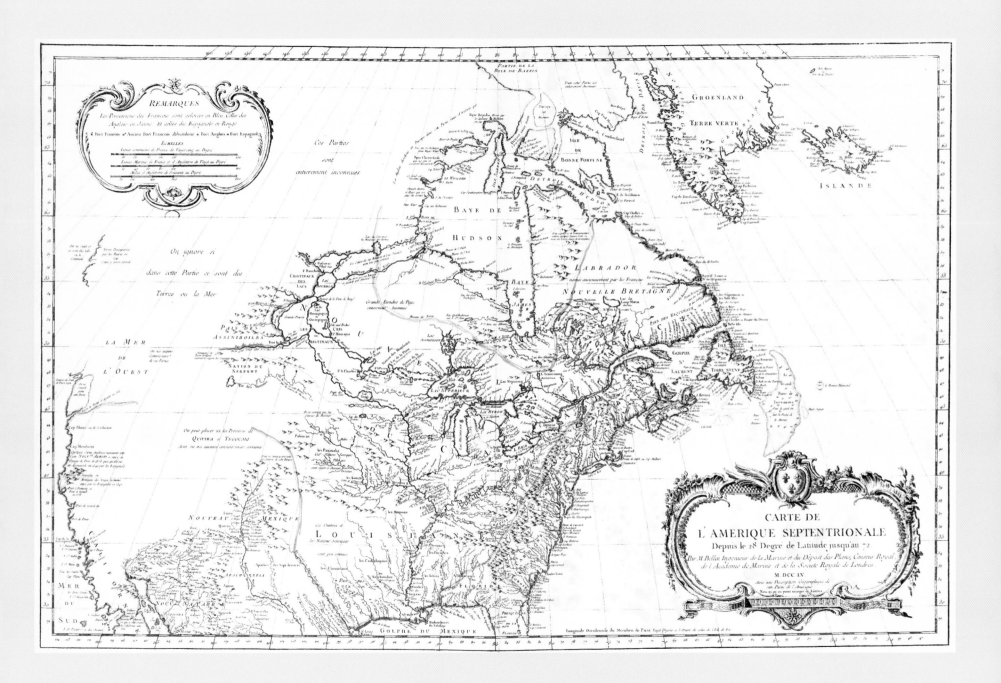

CARTE DE
L'AMERIQUE SEPTENTRIONALE
Depuis le 28 Degré de Latitude jusqu'au 72.
Par M. Bellin Ingenieur de la Marine et du Dépost des Plans, Censeur Royal
de l'Academie de Marine et de la Societe Royale de Londres.
M.DCC.LV.

III.

Albemarle Adventurers

By the mid-1700s, Virginia was fertile territory for land speculators and a breeding ground for exploration. The Governor and Council of Virginia, in an effort to extend the colony's borders and stake a legitimate claim to Western lands, began issuing large land grants to individuals and corporations to promote settlement in the uncharted West.

Members of the Virginia gentry who received these land grants were known as *adventurers*, a common term for the bold entrepreneurs or venture capitalists of the day. A group of Albemarle County adventurers launched the Loyal Company in 1749 to secure a large land patent and promote western colonization. This section examines several members of the Loyal Company and their connections with the Lewis and Clark Expedition.

In Virginia's hierarchical society, succeeding generations of the gentry, together with a group of lesser aristocracy and officeholders recruited from England, maintained their power and wealth in the colony through control of land, labor, and office holding. The gentry filled the rolls of the governor's council, the House of Burgesses, county offices, local parishes, and owned most of the land in the colony. Land was controlled through intermarriages and land grants from the governor's council. By the eighteenth century, many of the most prominent Virginia families were interrelated. The Meriwether and Lewis families, in fact, had intermarried eleven times.

Responding to the scarcity of land in the settled portion of the colony and pressure from the gentry, the Governor's Council began considering petitions for larger land grants along the western frontier. In 1730, Nicholas Meriwether II (1667-1744) received a grant of 17,952 acres along the Southwest Mountains. Meriwether Lewis's two grandfathers carved their plantations from this vast grant. The Jefferson property Pantops was originally part of a patent granted a group of men that included Jonathan Clark, the grandfather of William Clark. Shadwell, the birthplace of Thomas Jefferson, was part of a 1,000-acre grant to Jefferson's father, Peter, in 1735.

In order to manage their estates, identify resources, and control access to those resources, the Virginia gentry necessarily became proficient in the art of surveying and mapmaking. Knowledge of surveying gave Virginia's gentry inside information on choice new lands. George Washington, for example, chose surveying as a career, in part to insure that he would have access to the most desirable properties. When "laying off," or surveying, the bounty lands for services in the French and Indian War, Washington reserved the best lands for himself.

Prior to the Revolutionary War, parish vestry boards throughout Virginia appointed two freeholders from each precinct to verify property ownership and boundaries. This verification procedure was known as "processioning." Nicholas Meriwether II, Thomas Meriwether, Robert Lewis, and Thomas Walker were among those who served as Fredericksville Parish processioners. Vestry board members were also charged with surveying the changing parish and county lines and the property holdings of parish churches and glebes. Not surprisingly, skilled surveyors such as Joshua Fry, Peter Jefferson, and Thomas Walker also mapped land patents, frontier territories, and Virginia's boundaries.

Excitement for exploration of the West and speculative fervor dovetailed with Virginia's desire to extend its colonial boundaries. In 1749 a number of prominent Virginia adventurers established the Loyal Company to petition for a large grant of land west of the Allegheny Mountains. Charter members of the company included Peter Jefferson, Joshua Fry, Dr. Thomas Walker, James Maury, and Thomas Meriwether (Meriwether Lewis's grandfather). The company received a grant of 800,000 acres located along the southern border of Virginia (now southeastern Kentucky). The Loyal Company grant, the first vast land patent given to a corporation by the Governor and Council, contained a provision requiring settlement of the land within four years. Twice the company secured a renewal of the grant, but in 1763 the English crown rejected further extension of the grant as part of the ban on western settlements decreed by the Proclamation of 1763. Nevertheless, by this time the Loyal Company had completed many surveys of its land patent. While the Loyal Company faced numerous legal challenges to its holdings (the last in 1842), the courts upheld the company's land claims.

Shortly after its founding in 1749, the Loyal Company appointed Thomas Walker to lead an expedition to explore and survey its grant of 800,000 acres in what is now southeastern Kentucky. Dr. Thomas Walker (1715-1794) was a prominent resident of Louisa and Albemarle counties. A physician, surgeon, planter, trader, surveyor, cartographer, and explorer, Walker served in the House of Burgesses, in local government, and in the Fredericksville Parish. In 1741 he married Mildred Thornton, sister of Meriwether Lewis's maternal grandmother and widow of Nicholas Meriwether III (1699-1739). From this marriage Walker gained possession of large tracts of land along the Southwest Mountains—part of the large grant to Nicholas Meriwether II. Thomas Walker acted as executor of the estates of Meriwether Lewis's grandfather and Peter Jefferson and briefly served as Thomas Jefferson's guardian. In 1779 he served, along with Daniel Smith, as a Virginia Commissioner responsible for extending the Virginia-North Carolina border to the Mississippi River. He replaced John Lewis as head of the Loyal Company in 1753, holding the title of Agent of the company until his death in 1794. In 1750, a full seventeen years before Daniel Boone's legendary adventures in Kentucky, Thomas Walker traveled through the Cumberland Gap (which he named) and gathered geographical and topographical data as the first Virginian to explore the trans-Allegheny region.

Upon returning home, Walker produced a map from the information he gathered on his expedition into Kentucky. He presented the map to the House of Burgesses in 1769 during a debate over the boundary between Virginia's western settlements and Indian lands. George Washington, who was then head of the land-speculating Mississippi Company, modified Walker's map in 1769 and included it in that company's petition for 2.5 million acres near the junction of the Ohio and Mississippi rivers.

Walker's path-breaking expedition into the trans-Allegheny hinterland kindled the passions of the Virginia adventurers for more knowledge about the geography of the West. Members of the Loyal Company sought the latest reports of western exploration and shared accounts of exploration amongst themselves. The Reverend James Maury (1717-1769) read Joshua Fry's copy of Daniel Coxe's *A Description of the English Province of Carolana* (London, 1722), a book that espoused symmetrical geography (see pages 38-39). Maury, minister of the Fredericksville Parish from 1751 until 1769, was an enthusiastic student of the geography of North America. Coxe described a powerful Missouri River flowing into the Mississippi and providing an easy route to the Pacific Ocean. This "passage" to the West aroused the enthusiasm of Maury and other members of the Loyal Company.

A short time after the Loyal Company's expedition into Kentucky, several members of the Loyal Company proposed another expedition to explore the Missouri River and find a route to the Pacific Ocean. Thomas Walker was to lead the expedition, but the French and Indian War intervened and the scheme never came to fruition.

The Virginia gentry passed its interest in cartography, exploration, and western expansion down to younger generations through family and personal relationships. The West held a lifelong fascination for young Thomas Jefferson and Meriwether Lewis. Jefferson, who was ten years old in 1753, would likely have heard about the Loyal Company's western adventures from his father and from James Maury, his tutor for two years. Lewis also may have learned about the proposed expedition to the Pacific from his family or his personal tutor, James Maury's son, Matthew.

Joshua Fry (1700-1754), another Albemarle adventurer, was born in England, educated at Oxford, and taught mathematics at William and Mary College in Williamsburg before settling as a planter on the Hardware River south of Charlottesville around 1740. When Albemarle County was formed in 1744, he was appointed a county justice along with Peter Jefferson. Fry also served as presiding magistrate, county lieutenant, and county surveyor. Because of his surveying experience, he was designated a Crown Commissioner to establish the boundaries of the "Northern Neck," a proprietary grant of over five million acres.

On Fry's recommendation, Peter Jefferson became surveyor of the project. After the Council of State approved the completed survey in 1747, Fry and Peter Jefferson earned appointments as Virginia Commissioners to extend the boundary line between Virginia and North Carolina further westward. In 1751 Fry and Jefferson produced a new map of Virginia. Three years later Fry, while serving as Virginia's top colonial military leader, died of

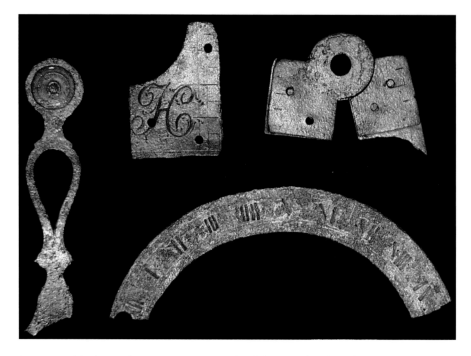

Fragments of drafting and surveying instruments found during archaeological excavations at Shadwell, birthplace of Thomas Jefferson. (Left) Brass arm from rectangular protractor. (Top center and right) Brass plate and hinge from wooden drafting scales. (Bottom) Fragment of brass dial ring from portable equatorial sundial, used by surveyors and travelers for telling time at any latitude. (Jesse Sawyer/Thomas Jefferson Foundation, Inc.)

injuries he received in a fall from his horse. Fry left his surveying instruments to Peter Jefferson in his will.

Peter Jefferson (1708-1757) was of Welsh descent and a man of legendary size and strength. Though lacking in formal education, he was well read and became a skilled surveyor and mapmaker. About 1735 he received a patent for 1,000 acres, to which he added 400 acres from William Randolph, his wife's kinsman. Peter Jefferson built his plantation Shadwell on this land, and his son Thomas was born there in 1743.

Peter Jefferson was one of the first residents of this Virginia frontier area. He became a justice of the peace, a county justice and sheriff, a lieutenant colonel in the militia, and he also represented his county in the House of Burgesses. In 1746 he and Thomas Lewis surveyed the "Fairfax Line," a task they completed only after undertaking an arduous expedition. Jefferson died in 1757, leaving behind his wife, six daughters, and two sons. In his will he left his surveying instruments and books to his son, Thomas.

Joshua Fry and Peter Jefferson.

"Map of the Inhabited part of Virginia, containing the whole
province of Maryland with Part of Pensilvania,
New Jersey and North Carolina." 1751.

Joshua Fry began petitioning the House of Burgesses for financial assistance to produce a new map of Virginia in 1738. His request was turned down four times until finally, in 1750, the Board of Trade and Plantations in England authorized the acting governor to appoint "the most proper and best qualified" surveyors to complete a new map. Joshua Fry and Peter Jefferson were commissioned to carry out this order. Although completed in 1751, the Fry-Jefferson map was not published until Thomas Jefferys of London issued it in 1754.

This first edition of the Fry-Jefferson map represents parts of the Middle Atlantic colonies from the Eastern seaboard to the Ohio River. It accurately depicts the settled parts of Virginia and is the first map to show the Appalachian Mountains running in the correct direction. Longitude is shown in degrees west from a line extending from Philadelphia to Currituck Inlet. The area to the west of the mountains has several errors: Lake Erie is erroneously located two hundred miles further south than it belongs and the Ohio River is distorted. The map shown here is one of only four known copies of the first edition.

The second edition of the Fry-Jefferson map, published in 1755, corrected many of the problems of the original by drawing on data collected by Fry, George Washington, and others. Also in 1755, John Evans used this updated map in preparing his own seminal map of North America, "Map of the Middle British Colonies." Evans credited the reliability of the Fry-Jefferson map, "as this had the assistance of actual surveys . . . joined to the Experi-ence of two skillful Persons." Similarly, Gilles Robert de Vaugondy, geographer to the king of France, used a modified version of the Fry-Jefferson map in his 1756 atlas. Both the British and French consulted the map during the French and Indian War and the American Revolution. The map went through several editions, the last published in 1794. Thomas Jefferson used the Fry-Jefferson map in drawing his map for *Notes on the State of Virginia*.

(*Special Collections, University of Virginia Library*)

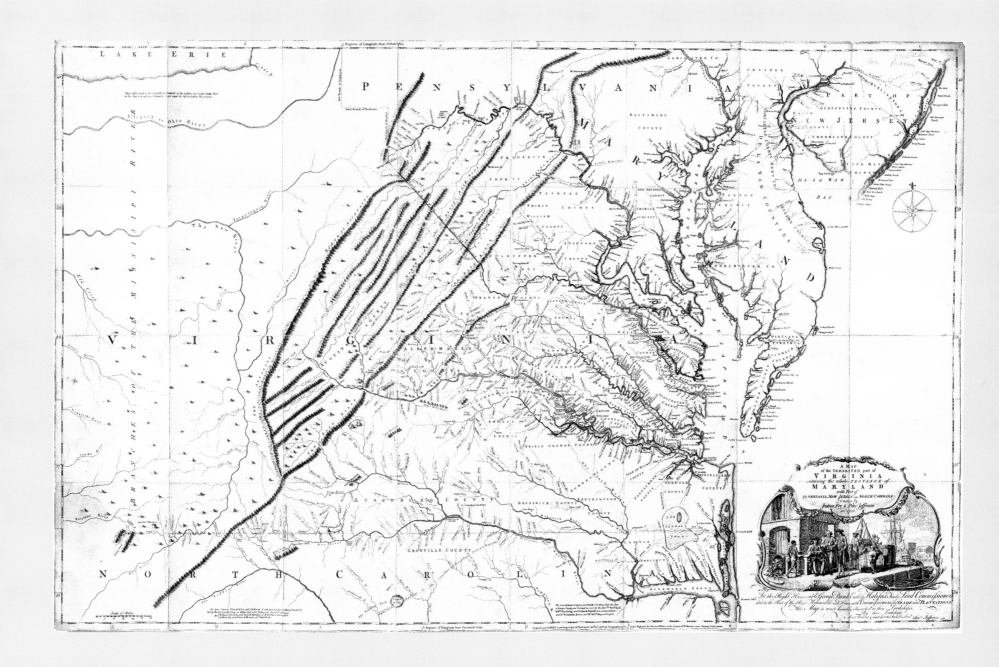

LAKE ERIE

PENSYLVANIA

MARYLAND

NEW JERSEY

DE LA WAR

VIRGINIA

BRANCHES OF THE MISSISIPI RIVER

NORTH CAROLINA

A MAP
of the INHABITED part of
VIRGINIA
containing the whole PROVINCE of
MARYLAND
with Part of
PENSILVANIA, NEW JERSEY and NORTH CAROLINA
Drawn by
Joshua Fry & Peter Jefferson
in 1751

Thomas Jefferson.

"A Map of the country between Albemarle Sound, and
   Lake Erie, comprehending the whole of Virginia,
   Maryland, Delaware and Pensylvania, with parts of
   several other of the United States of America."
In *Notes on the State of Virginia*. London, 1787.

Thomas Jefferson's (1743-1826) avid interest in geography and cartography was evident in his lifelong quest for knowledge about Virginia and the western regions of North America. His enthusiasm for maps probably came from the formative influences of his father, his tutor Reverend James Maury, and other members of the Loyal Company. Like his elders, Thomas Jefferson was a practicing surveyor. More importantly, he amassed a collection of 350 atlases and books on geography-related topics and over one hundred printed and manuscript maps. Although he never traveled west of Warm Springs, Virginia, he is generally believed to be the most knowledgeable person of his time on the geography of the western part of North America.

Despite his breadth of knowledge and talents as a writer, Thomas Jefferson published only one book—*Notes on the State of Virginia*. This work began as a response to a detailed questionnaire on the conditions of North America sent by the French Legation in 1780 to all the former British colonies. Jefferson expanded his response over several years into a compendium on the natural history and geographical, social, political, and economic characteristics of Virginia and other parts of America. Although Jefferson apparently never intended to publish this material, he did circulate a few privately printed copies to selected individuals, which led to an unauthorized and inaccurate French translation in 1785. Jefferson finally approved the official release of the book in French and English editions in 1787. He continued to revise the manuscript until 1814, although he never issued a revised version.

Jefferson prepared a map for his book based on the map co-authored by his father (republished in 1774), a map by Thomas Hutchins published in 1778, and a map of Pennsylvania by William Scull published in 1770. When he sent his map to the engraver in England, he listed those maps and Henry Mouzon's map of North Carolina as references. Jefferson added "A Map of the Country between Albemarle Sound, and Lake Erie" to *Notes on the State of Virginia* and also issued the map separately.

(The Tracy W. McGregor Library of American History, Special Collections, University of Virginia Library)

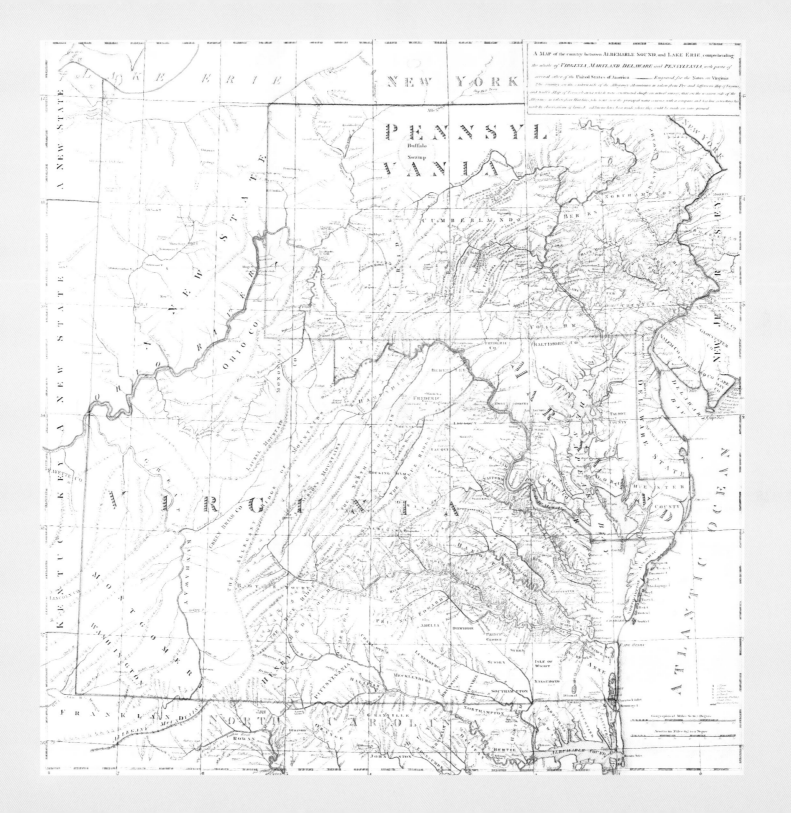

IV.

To the Western Ocean: Planning the Lewis and Clark Expedition

In the latter half of the eighteenth century, English, Spanish, and American explorers replaced their French counterparts as the leaders of exploration in the Mississippi and Missouri river valleys. As before, sensational accounts of western voyages continued to generate interest in the region. Widely read works by Antoine-Simon Le Page du Pratz, Robert Rogers, and Jonathan Carver enriched the tradition of popular reporting about the West. Increasingly, however, improved scientific methods of surveying, cartography, and natural description allowed for a more accurate picture of the geography of the West. By the end of the century the exact latitudes and longitudes of several important points in the West had been determined. The latest maps and journals of the explorers and cartographers influenced significantly the planning of the Lewis and Clark Expedition.

The exploration of the Missouri and Mississippi valleys proceeded slowly after the French ceded Louisiana to Spain in 1764. In fact, following Bourgmont's expedition in 1714, no European successfully ascended the Missouri River much beyond the Platte River until Jacques D'Église reached the Mandan Indian villages (in the present-day Washburn-Stanton area of North Dakota) in 1791. D'Église brought back stories of incursions by English traders into upper Louisiana from Canada. Alarmed at these threats to its sovereignty in the region, Spain took steps to promote the exploration of the upper Missouri River. In 1793, the Spanish chartered a "Company of Discoverers and Explorers of the Missouri," or Missouri Company, to exploit the fur trade on the upper Missouri. The Spanish crown offered a prize to the first

Spanish subject to reach the Pacific Ocean via the Missouri River and sponsored separate expeditions to the Mandan villages by Jean-Baptiste Truteau, Antoine Simon Lecuyer de la Jonchère, and James Mackay in 1794 and 1795. Finally, in 1796, a party sent by Mackay under John Evans succeeded in reaching those villages.

In the lore of American exploration, the idea of finding a great river leading from the Pacific coast to the interior of the continent never lost currency. Mapmakers had long postulated a great "River of the West," or "Oregan River," as it was also called. Martin d'Aguilar of Spain was probably the first European to see the Columbia River in 1603, but his claims remained unsubstantiated for nearly 175 years. Upon reaching turbulent waters along the Northwest coast in 1775, another Spaniard, Bruno de Hezeta, said, "These currents and eddies of water cause me to believe that the place is the mouth of some great river, or of some passage to another sea." And yet, the river proved elusive. The greatest English explorer of all, Captain James Cook, missed the Columbia River entirely during his voyages along the West coast in 1778.

Although Cook failed to find the Columbia River, his voyage to the Pacific Northwest was not without bold ramifications for the exploration and development of the West coast. From his astronomical observations, Cook determined the width of the North American continent. He also discovered a very profitable sea otter trade, which sparked a heated competition among England, Spain, France, Russia, and the newly independent United States for a foothold on the West coast. In 1785, King Louis XVI of France sent the famous sea hero Jean-François de Galaup, comte de La Pérouse, to probe the Pacific coast of America and find a propitious site for a fur trading post. George Vancouver and Alexander Mackenzie, representing Britain, and Robert Gray of the United States explored the Pacific Northwest shortly thereafter. Thanks to the efforts of these explorers, the Northwest coastline was surveyed and mapped before 1800.

Meanwhile, in Canada, independent traders who later organized as the North West Company pushed westward to preclude the involvement of the Hudson's Bay Company in the fur trade in western Canada. Finally, in 1793, Alexander Mackenzie, a member of the North West Company, reached the Pacific Ocean, completing the first overland journey to the Pacific north of Mexico. In 1798 David Thompson, a cartographer with the North West Company, mapped part of the upper Missouri for the first time and determined the latitude and longitude of the Great Bend of the Missouri (see pages 76-77).

This surge in exploration provided considerable new geographic information on the Missouri and Columbia river basins. Although the expeditions of the late 1700s were primarily motivated by commercial and nationalistic concerns, they also renewed interest in a route to the Pacific and in geographical theories such as symmetrical geography, pyramidal height-of-land, and the continental divide.

Perhaps no American felt this romantic yearning for the West more powerfully than Thomas Jefferson. The elders of Jefferson's social circle had planned an expedition to the Pacific. Sharing his father's avid interest in cartography, Thomas Jefferson followed the reports of the explorations of the late 1700s very closely and collected many of the newly published journals and maps. Indeed, Jefferson himself promoted three unsuccessful attempts to find a route to the Pacific: in 1783 by George Rogers Clark (the brother of William Clark); in 1787-1788 by John Ledyard; and in 1793 by André Michaux.

In the summer of 1802, Jefferson, during his first term as president of the United States, read Alexander Mackenzie's account of his journey through the North American continent to the Pacific. Mackenzie's recommendation that the British government assume control of the Columbia River troubled Jefferson, who feared for the national interest if the British appropriated the West coast and all avenues inland. In response, Jefferson organized a bold new national enterprise to reach the Pacific. After Congress approved his plan for an expedition, Jefferson appointed his secretary Meriwether Lewis to lead the exploring party, later known as the "Corps of Discovery."

Meriwether Lewis, who had gained firsthand knowledge of the western frontier in the military, was an Albemarle County neighbor of Thomas Jefferson. Lewis's grandfather, Thomas Meriwether, and Jefferson's father had each been members of the Loyal Company. In 1803 Jefferson dispatched Lewis north to Pennsylvania to make arrangements for the expedition and to augment his training in geography and cartography. Both Jefferson and Lewis realized the urgency of this training, since the expedition would offer an unprecedented chance to collect data on the geography of the western half of the American continent. Thus, before commencing the expedition, Lewis learned how to make celestial observations from Robert Patterson, a mathematician, and Andrew Ellicott, the foremost American geographer and surveyor of his day.

In August 1803 Lewis set off down the Ohio River from Pittsburgh and stopped at Louisville, Kentucky, to see his friend and newly appointed expedition co-captain, William Clark. Lewis carried along various explorer's accounts and maps of the West, including geographical works by Arrowsmith, Mackenzie, Vancouver, Thompson, and Le Page du Pratz, as well as reference books and astronomical tables for making longitudinal calculations. At some

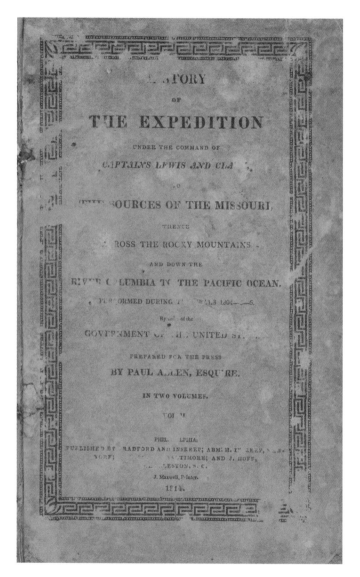

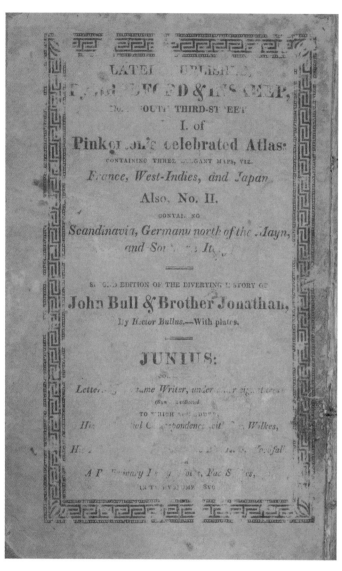

The 1814 History of the Expedition under the Command of Captains Lewis and Clark *expedition journals in original boards.*
(The Paul Mellon Collection, Special Collections, University of Virginia Library)

point he also received a new map by Nicholas King (page 81) that Secretary of the Treasury Albert Gallatin had commissioned expressly for the expedition.

While at Camp Dubois near St. Louis during the winter of 1804, Lewis and Clark obtained additional maps by James Mackay and Antoine Soulard, a series of route maps by John Evans, excerpts from Jean-Baptiste Truteau's journal, and the journal of Mackay and Evans. Lewis spent a great deal of time in and around St. Louis talking to Indian traders who had knowledge of the Missouri River. That same winter, Clark, an experienced surveyor, taught himself how to use the sextant and the octant that Lewis had acquired for the expedition. Clark, in fact, performed most of the expedition's mapping duties.

Both Meriwether Lewis and William Clark continued to learn about the topography of the West from Indians and traders as they ascended the Missouri River throughout 1804 and at their winter camp near the Mandan villages. Like other explorers before them, they made extensive use of Indian maps, which were drawn on animal skins or sketched from scratchings in the dirt.

This section focuses on the explorations and maps of the West that immediately preceded the departure of Meriwether Lewis from the East in 1803. Geographic information from British, French, and American explorations in the West and along the Pacific coast shaped Thomas Jefferson's planning of the Lewis and Clark Expedition, but Jefferson apparently knew little about the Spanish-sponsored explorations of the 1790s. The final items in this section show the results of the Lewis and Clark Expedition: William Clark's map of 1810 (page 83), an engraved version of which later appeared in the 1814 published journals of the expedition (see pages 84-85).

John Mitchell.

"A Map of the British and French Dominions in North
America with the Roads, Distances, Limits, and Extent
of the Settlements." 1755.
Southwestern quadrant.

John Mitchell (1711-1768) enjoyed a remarkably varied and distin-
guished career as a physician, botanist, chemist, biologist, and surveyor.
Mitchell lived for a time in Virginia but he immigrated to England in 1746
and remained there until his death. In 1750, the president of the Board of
Trade and Plantations commissioned Mitchell to prepare a map of the British
colonies in North America to stretch and strengthen Britain's territorial
claims in the West. Drawing on the archives of the British government,
Mitchell worked for five years on this project, which he called "A Map of the
British and French Dominions in North America with the Roads, Distances,
Limits, and Extent of the Settlements." True to his instructions, Mitchell ex-
tended the boundaries of Virginia, both Carolinas, and Georgia across the
Mississippi River.

*(The Tracy W. McGregor Library of American History, Special Collections,
University of Virginia Library)*

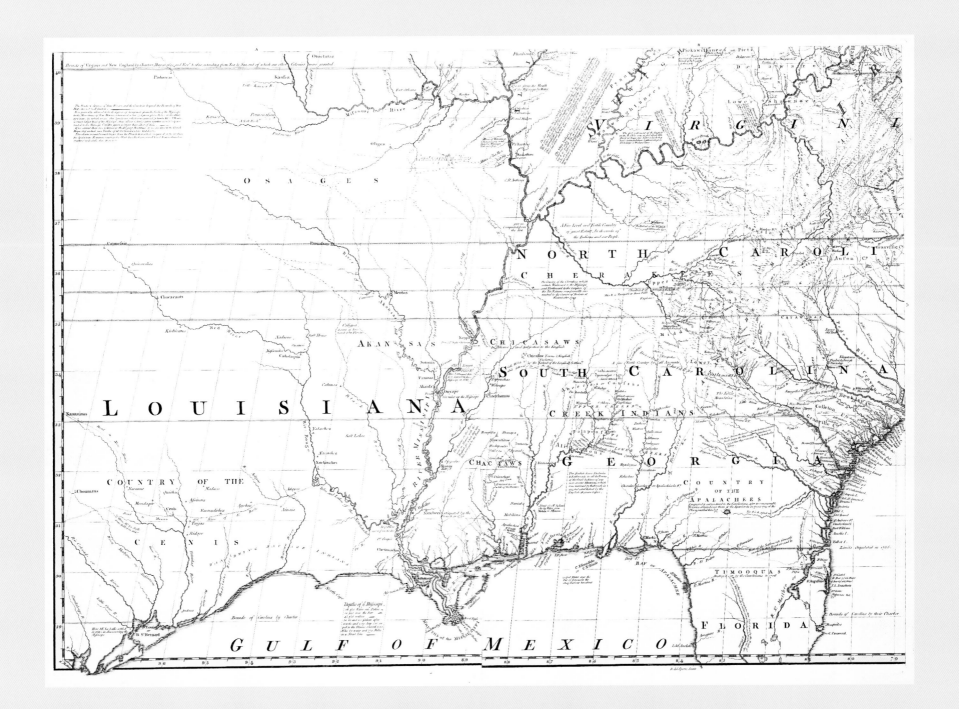

John Mitchell.

"A Map of the British and French Dominions in North
America with the Roads, Distances, Limits, and Extent
of the Settlements." 1755.
Northwestern quadrant.

In its treatment of the West, John Mitchell's map depicts the lower Missouri more accurately than any other map of the time. Mitchell did not indicate the source of the Missouri, although his notation, "Missouri river is reckoned to run Westward to the Mountains of New Mexico, as far as the Ohio does Eastward," suggests his belief in symmetrical geography. Mitchell correctly shows the northern branch of the Missouri to be the main branch of the river, although his estimate of the latitude of the river's source is inaccurate. Nonetheless, the information Mitchell's map provided led Meriwether Lewis up the Marias River to determine the northern reaches of the Missouri River basin.

Although Mitchell never produced another map, "A Map of the British and French Dominions" is one of the most significant maps in American history. It was the only map used during the peace negotiations between Great Britain and the former American colonies that culminated in the Treaty of Paris. The map helped settle many subsequent treaty negotiations and boundary disputes, the last in 1932. Thomas Jefferson recommended that Nicholas King use Mitchell's map as he prepared a new map for Meriwether Lewis, saying: "it was made with great care we know from what is laid down in those western parts with which we have lately become acquainted."

Mitchell's map went through twenty-one editions and impressions to 1791. Special Collections owns several editions and impressions of "A Map of the British and French Dominions in North America," including a third impression of the first English edition (1755), shown here.

(The Tracy W. McGregor Library of American History, Special Collections, University of Virginia Library)

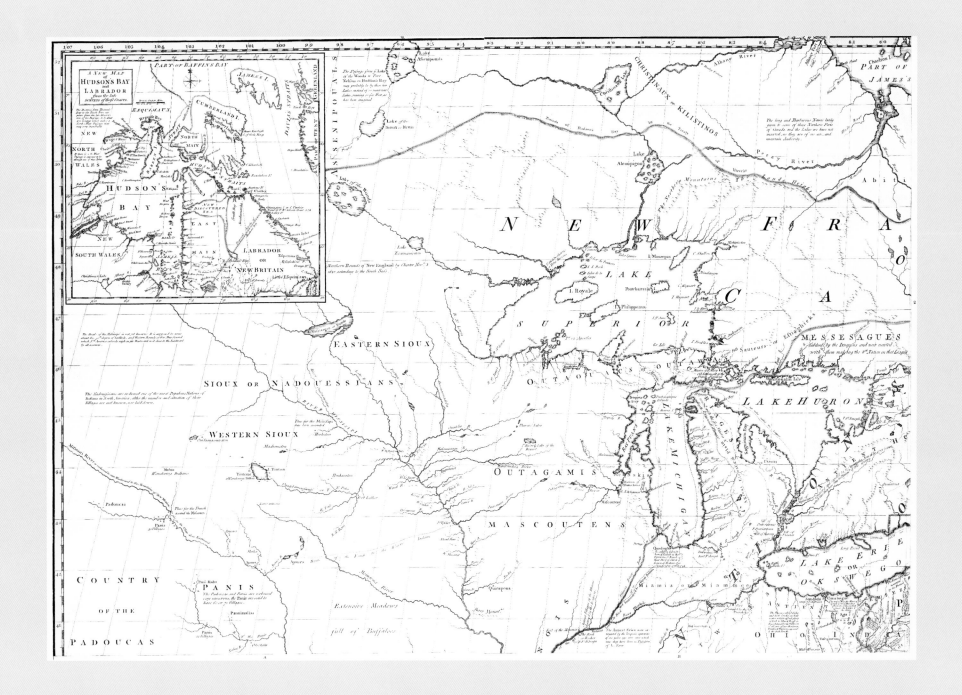

Antoine-Simon Le Page du Pratz.

"A Map of Louisiana, with the course of the Missisipi."
In *The History of Louisiana, or of the western parts of Virginia and Carolina.* London, 1763.

The French military engineer Antoine-Simon Le Page du Pratz (c.1695-1775) came to North America in 1718 and spent fifteen years as a planter in Louisiana. During this period he made a five-month tour of the interior of Louisiana. Drawing on information received from Étienne Venyard, sieur de Bourgmont, a contemporary explorer of the region, he wrote *Histoire de la Louisiane* (Paris, 1758), which presents the first published account of Bourgmont's expedition to the Padouca Indians, or Plains Apaches, in 1724. Le Page du Pratz borrowed liberally from the writings of Charlevoix and from Dumont de Montigny's *Mémoires historiques sur la Louisiane* (Paris, 1753). *Histoire de la Louisiane* contains a map entitled "Carte de la Louisiane Colonie Française avec le Cours du Fleuve St. Louis."

Le Page du Pratz's map depicts the lower Mississippi and lower Missouri rivers fairly accurately, although it mistakenly shows the Missouri River flowing from the west unimpeded by any mountains. This representation was consistent with the widely held belief that the source of the Missouri was near the source of the Rio Grande. Le Page du Pratz estimated the length of the lower Missouri to be nearly 2,400 miles; the actual distance from the mouth of the Missouri to the Three Forks of the Missouri in present-day Montana is 2,547 miles.

Note that the map includes Lahontan's system of rivers and lakes in the North, although it labels the river running westward toward the Pacific the "Beautiful River." In his book, Le Page du Pratz tells of an Indian who discovered a route to the Pacific Ocean via the Beautiful River. The Indian's path from the Missouri to the Beautiful River is shown on the map.

"A Map of Louisiana, with the course of the Missisipi" is included in the first English edition of Le Page du Pratz's book, *The History of Louisiana, or of the western parts of Virginia and Carolina* (London, 1763). Thomas Jefferson owned this edition of the work and used it as a reference source as he prepared his treatise on Louisiana. Meriwether Lewis borrowed the English edition from Benjamin Smith Barton, his botany tutor in Philadelphia, and took it on the expedition to the Pacific. Several references to Le Page du Pratz's work appear in the journals of the expedition. A shorter version of the work, entitled "From a Memoir of M. Le Page du Pratz," appeared in *Gentleman's Magazine* in 1753.

(The Tracy W. McGregor Library of American History, Special Collections, University of Virginia Library)

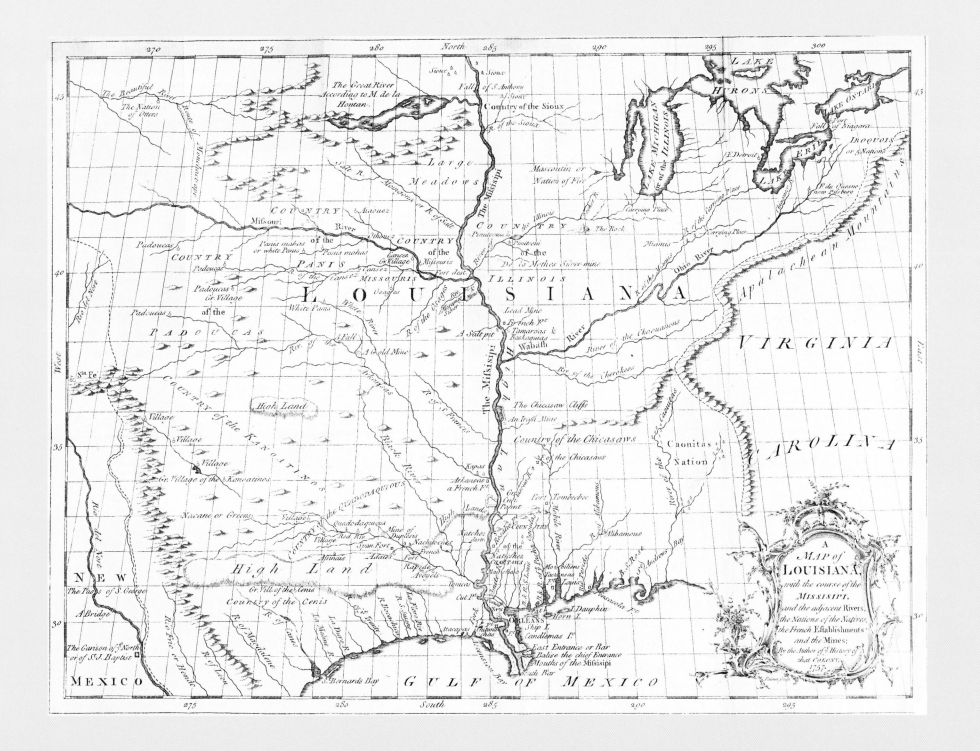

270   275   280   North   285   290   295   300

45

The Beautiful River Route of *Hontan*

The Nation of Otters

Sioux Sioux

The Great River According to M. de la Hontan.

Fall of *S.* Anthony

Country of the Sioux

R. of the Sioux

LAKE HURONS

LAKE MICHIGAN or of the ILLINOIS

LAKE ERIE

LAKE ONTARIO

Fall of Niagara Fort

IROQUOIS or 5 Nations

F. Detroit

F. du Quesne now Pitsburg

Large Meadows

Mascoutin or Nation of Fire

Salt R.

COUNTRY

Aiaouez

Missouri River of the

PANIS

Panis mahas or white Panis

Panis mahas

COUNTRY of the

Missouris

MISSOURIS

Fort dest.

COUNTRY of the

ILLINOIS

R. of the Illinois

Pimiteoui L.

River of Pimiteoui

The Rock

De la Mothes Silver mine

Miamis

Ohio River

R. of the Miamis

Carrying Place

Carrying Place

Apalachean Mountains

VIRGINIA

40

Padoucas

COUNTRY

Padoucas

Padoucas Gr. Village

Padoucas of the

PADOUCAS

Of the Cansez

Cansez Gr. Village

Osages

White Panis

R. of the Osages

Missouri River

LOUISIANA

Lead Mine

French Ft.

Tamaroas & Kaskaquias

Wabash

River of the Choouanons

Riv of the Cherokees

R. of the Ohio

40

Rio del Norte

R. of the Cansez

White River

A Salt pit

A Gold Mine

The Missisipi

The Missisipi

River

35

Sta Fe

COUNTRY of the Kanontinos

High Land

R. of the Franco

Arkansas

Black River

The Chicasaw Cliffs

An Irish Mine

Country of the Chicasaws

Caonitas Nation

R. of the Caonitas

CAROLINA

35

Village

Village

Village

Gr. Village of the Kanoatinos

Nacane or Greens

Village

COUNTRY of the QUADODAQUIOUS

Village

Quadodaquious

Kapas

Arkansas a French Ft.

High Land

F. of the Chicasaws

Fort Tombecbec

Mobile River

R. Alibamous

R. Alibamous

30

Rio del Norte

The Passes of S. George

A Bridge

The Garison of y. North or of S. J. Baptist

Rio Frio or Leon

R. of Macdalene

High Land

Country of the Cenis

Gr. Vill. of the Cenis

R. of Trane

R. of Trinity

La Fere R.

R. Blanche

R. Rouge

Ascension Bay of the

S. Bernards Bay

Asinais

Adais

Village

Red Riv.

Mine of Duplesis

Nachitoches

Span Fort

Rapide

Avoyels

Tomicas

Natchez destr.

Country of the Natchez

Macapas

Fork

Bayouc ou Chas

New ORLEANS

Fort Pondes.

R. of S.t Louis

Moschitiens Tixemenas Ft.

S.t Louis

Pascagola R.

B.y Pascela

B.y Rose

R.y S.t Andrews

Mobile Bay

Pensacola Ft.

I. Dauphin

Horn I.

Ship I.

Candlemas I.

East Entrance or Bar

Balise the chief Entrance

Mouths of the Missisipi

S.t Bernards Bay

NEW MEXICO

GULF OF MEXICO

30

A
MAP of
LOUISIANA,
with the course of the
MISSISIPI,
and the adjacent Rivers,
the Nations of the Natives,
the French Establishments
and the Mines;
By the Author of y.ᵉ History of
that COLONY.
1757.

275   280   South   285   290   295

Jonathan Carver.

"A New Map of North America From the Latest Discoveries."
In *Travels Through the Interior Parts of North America in the
Years 1766, 1767, and 1768.* London, 1781.

Massachusetts-born explorer Jonathan Carver (1710-1780) assisted in the efforts of Robert Rogers (1727-1795) to find a route to the Pacific Ocean. Rogers, a soldier and adventurer who never traveled to either the Missouri or the upper Mississippi rivers, nonetheless published a book in 1765 describing the Mississippi River and the major rivers that flow into it. In 1766 Rogers sent Carver to map the upper Mississippi basin in preparation for a western expedition. Carver crossed Lake Michigan, traversed the Fox and Wisconsin rivers to the Mississippi, and then traveled up the St. Peter River, or Minnesota River. He was the first English-speaking explorer to venture west of the upper Mississippi River. After wintering with the Sioux Indians, Carver backtracked the next spring to Prairie du Chien (in present-day Wisconsin), where he met the expedition sent by Rogers. When supplies failed to arrive, however, the expedition was abandoned.

In 1769 Carver went to England, where he published an account of his travels, *Travels Through the Interior Parts of North America in the Years 1766, 1767, and 1768* (London, 1778). Carver's book is notable for endorsing the height-of-land theory and anticipating the idea of a continental divide. According to Carver,

> The four most capital rivers on the Continent of North America, viz. the St. Lawrence, the Mississippi, the River Bourbon [today, the Nelson River], and the Oregon or the River of the West, . . . have their sources in the same neighborhood. The waters of the three former are within thirty miles of each other; the latter, however is rather further west.

Carver's map shows the "Mantons R.," or the upper Missouri, starting near the sources of a truncated Missouri River and the Mississippi River. The "Mantons R." flows westward to "Pikes Lake," which is connected by a dotted line to the "River of the West." While this route represents a convenient passage to the Northwest, Carver's book is the first to mention a large mountain range to the south (presumably the Rocky Mountains) that blocks the westward passage and serves as a continental divide.

The map shown here is included in the third English edition (1781) of *Travels Through the Interior Parts of North America.* Carver's best-selling book was published in more than thirty editions. Thomas Jefferson owned a 1797 edition. The book brought the word Oregon into popular use and expanded on the notion of the *noble savage* then gaining acceptance in European literary circles. Carver borrowed extensively from earlier books by Hennepin, Lahontan, and Charlevoix. Some critics doubted the authenticity of Carver's observations and speculated that his travel journal was actually the work of another explorer. A 1792 letter to the American geographer Jedediah Morse claimed that Carver "doubtless resided a number of years in the western country, but was an ignorant man, utterly incapable of writing such a book."

(The Tracy W. McGregor Library of American History, Special Collections, University of Virginia Library)

James Cook.

"Chart of the NW Coast of America and NE Coast of Asia
explored in the years 1778 and 1779."
In *A Voyage to the Pacific Ocean*. London, 1784.

James Cook (1728-1779) was Britain's greatest navigator. After receiving a modest education, he developed a love for the sea while apprenticing at a small shop on the Yorkshire coast. Cook enlisted in the Royal Navy in 1755. Sent to America during the French and Indian War, he made soundings of the St. Lawrence River in preparation for the British attack on Quebec. Cook's notable charts of the St. Lawrence earned him a commission as surveyor of Newfoundland. In 1768 he was promoted and sent to the Pacific, where he surveyed Tahiti, New Zealand, and Australia. On his famous second expedition (1772-1775) he explored Antarctica. He undertook his third and final voyage in 1776, exploring the West coast of North America and trying to locate a passage between the Atlantic and Pacific oceans. On this voyage he discovered the Hawaiian Islands (which he named the Sandwich Islands) and sailed up the coast of North America through the Bering Straits to the Arctic Ocean. He concluded that a usable passage to the Atlantic Ocean did not exist. On his return to the Pacific he was killed by Hawaiian islanders.

Cook's exploration of the Pacific coast of North America was at once momentous and fraught with errors. He missed the mouth of the Columbia River (then known as the Oregan River or River of the West), as well as the Juan de Fuca Strait, a passage into Puget Sound. He also mistook Vancouver Island for the mainland. Despite these oversights, Cook's third voyage significantly increased knowledge of and interest in the Northwest. His chart of the Pacific coast served as a chief reference source for Nicholas King as he prepared a new map of America for the Lewis and Clark Expedition in 1803 (page 81). More significantly, Cook's widely read firsthand accounts provided fascinating descriptions of the indigenous peoples in the Pacific Northwest and publicized the brisk trade between the Hudson's Bay Company and the Indians. Cook's almost incidental discovery of the sea otter trade—he found that the furs of the region's abundant sea otters brought enormous profits in the markets of Canton, China—sparked a race to the Pacific Northwest. Upon the 1783 publication of an unofficial account of Cook's third voyage and the release of the official account the following year, Britain, France, and the new United States joined Spain and Russia in the contest for control of the Pacific Northwest and the sea otter trade.

After Cook's third voyage, one of his sailors, the American John Ledyard, wrote an unofficial account of the journey. Ledyard tried, unsuccessfully, to raise a fur-trading expedition to the Northwest in 1784-1785. In 1785 he met Thomas Jefferson and the two quickly became friends. Jefferson, then ambassador to France, owned three unofficial versions of *Cook's Third Voyage*, including Ledyard's, as well as the official account of 1784. These accounts, as well as the renewal of French interest in the Pacific Northwest signaled by La Pérouse's expedition of 1785, strengthened Jefferson's commitment to find a path to the Pacific. Jefferson, in fact, sponsored Ledyard's bizarre expedition of 1787-1788 to cross Russia, travel to the Northwest coast of North America by ship, and then find a route to the Missouri by traveling from west to east. Ledyard got as far as Siberia before being arrested by Russian authorities under Catherine the Great.

(Special Collections, University of Virginia Library)

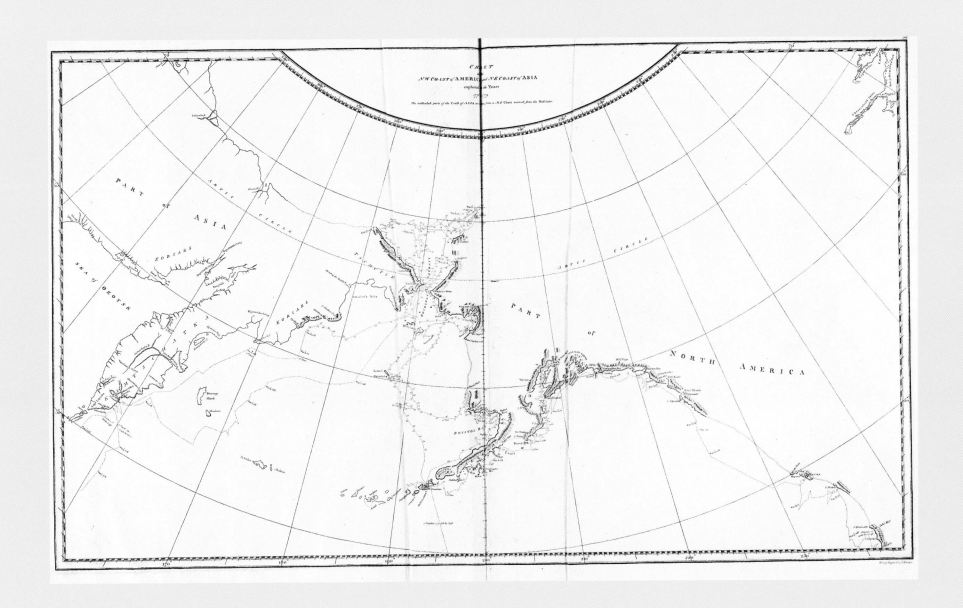

Chart
N.W. COAST of AMERICA and N.E. COAST of ASIA
explored in the Years
1778 & 1779
The unshaded parts of the Coast of ASIA are taken from a M.S. Chart received from the Russians.

George Vancouver.

"A Chart Shewing Part of the Coast of N.W. America."
In *A Voyage of discovery to the North Pacific ocean, and Round the World*. London, 1798.

English navigator and explorer George Vancouver (1758-1798) entered the Royal Navy in 1771 upon receiving an appointment from Captain James Cook. He accompanied Cook on his voyage around the world in 1772-1774 and served as a midshipman on Cook's explorations along the West coast of North America. Vancouver was promoted to commander of the ship *Discovery* in 1790. The next year he embarked on a multi-faceted mission to receive the surrender of the Spanish post at Nootka Sound in present-day British Columbia, survey the coast of the American Northwest, and search for a water connection to the eastern part of the continent. Equipped with the best navigational instruments of his day, Vancouver and his well-trained men spent three years surveying the coast. He produced superb charts of the Northwest coast of America and wrote a lengthy account of his voyage, *A Voyage of discovery to the North Pacific ocean, and Round the World* (1798). The map shown here is from the atlas that accompanied Vancouver's book.

Vancouver, like Cook before him, initially missed the Columbia River on his voyages along the coast. The commander of the *Discovery* refused to believe an American sea captain in the vicinity who described his attempt to enter the mouth of a great river. A few weeks after this meeting, the American captain, Robert Gray, returned to the scene of his previous efforts and on May 12, 1792, became the first explorer to enter the Columbia River by crossing over the sandbar that blocked its mouth. Gray sailed about twenty miles up the estuary of the river, traded with the Indians for a few days, and then left after drawing a chart of the mouth of the river. He named the river

the Columbia after his ship, and claimed it for the United States.

George Vancouver obtained a copy of Gray's chart from the Spanish governor at Nootka Sound and sailed to the mouth of the Columbia River in October 1792. Although Vancouver was unable to get his flagship *Discovery* over the sandbar, Lieutenant William Robert Broughton succeeded with his smaller ship, the *HMS Chatham*. Broughton advanced nearly 100 miles to a site opposite present-day Portland, Oregon, which he named Point Vancouver. To the east he saw a majestic mountain peak, which he named Mount Hood. Broughton erroneously believed that a single range of mountains to the east functioned as a continental divide; this belief was consistent with Alexander Mackenzie's contemporary account.

The reports of Vancouver and Broughton of a navigable Columbia River and a continental divide encouraged Thomas Jefferson and others who planned Lewis and Clark's westward crossing of the continent. Since Vancouver's publication was too bulky to carry on the expedition, Meriwether Lewis traced Vancouver's charts so that he could have them on the voyage. In addition, Nicholas King relied on Vancouver's charts when preparing his map for the expedition (page 81). The accurate chart of the lower Columbia that Broughton had produced for Vancouver proved especially useful to Lewis and Clark as they approached the Pacific coast.

(The Tracy W. McGregor Library of American History, Special Collections, University of Virginia Library)

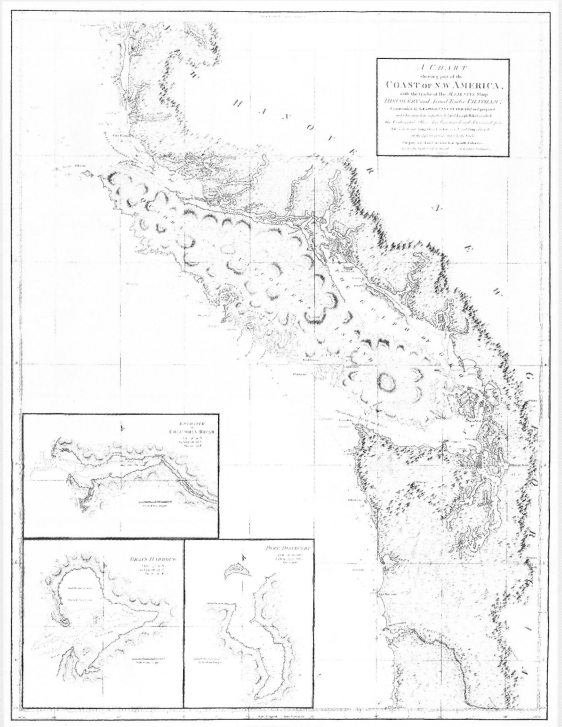

A CHART
showing part of the
COAST of N.W. AMERICA,
with the tracks of His MAJESTY's Sloop
DISCOVERY and Armed Tender CHATHAM;
Commanded by GEORGE VANCOUVER Esqr. and prepared
under his immediate inspection by Lieut. Joseph Baker, in which
the Continental Shore has been traced and determined from
Lat. 30° 0′ 0″ and Long. 236° 0′ 0″ and Long. 232° 0″
at the figures are as shown in the Study.

ENTRANCE
of
COLUMBIA RIVER

GRAY'S HARBOUR

PORT DISCOVERY

Alexander Mackenzie.

"A Map of America between Latitudes 40 and 70 North, and
Longitudes 45 and 180 West, Exhibiting Mackenzie's
Track."
In *Voyages from Montreal, on the River St. Laurence, through
the Continent of North America to the Frozen and Pacific
Oceans; In the Years 1789 and 1793.* London, 1801.

Scottish-born fur trader and explorer Alexander Mackenzie (1763-1820) commanded Fort Chipewyan on Lake Athabasca in present-day Alberta for the North West Company from 1788 to 1796. During this time he made voyages to the Arctic and Pacific oceans. Between these explorations he went to England to study navigational science. In 1801 he returned to London to publish *Voyages from Montreal, on the River St. Laurence, through the Continent of North America*, which chronicled his exploits in western Canada. After being knighted for his achievements in exploration, Mackenzie acted as a statesman in urging Britain to assert control over the Pacific Northwest.

Mackenzie was the second explorer to reach Lake Athabasca and the Great Slave Lake in the present-day Northwest Territories of Canada. He not only followed the American Peter Pond to Lake Athabasca, he also based his route to the Pacific on Pond's prediction that a river led from the Great Slave Lake to the Pacific Ocean. In 1789, Mackenzie followed this river (which later bore his name), only to reach the Arctic Ocean instead of the Pacific. Four years later he ascended the Peace River before crossing over the Continental Divide to the Fraser River—a river he believed to be the upper reaches of the Columbia River and labeled the "Tacoutche Tesse or Columbia River" on his map. Mackenzie completed his journey in July 1793 by traveling over land another fourteen days to the Pacific Ocean at present-day Bella Coola,

British Columbia. Mackenzie thus became the first European to reach the Pacific coast north of Mexico by traveling from the east.

Thomas Jefferson was aware of Mackenzie's success at least as early as 1797, although he did not read the detailed account of his voyage until the summer of 1802. Jefferson's attention doubtlessly would have been drawn to Mackenzie's description of an easy crossing of the Continental Divide. Mackenzie's claim that he traveled on a path that was only "eight hundred and seventeen paces in length over a ridge of 3000 ft. elevation" and his report that the mountains to the south were of even lower elevation convinced Jefferson of the feasibility of an American expedition across the continent. Moreover, Mackenzie's urgent recommendations that the British government secure control of the Pacific Northwest probably hastened President Jefferson's authorization of an expedition to the Northwest.

(The Tracy W. McGregor Library of American History, Special Collections, University of Virginia Library)

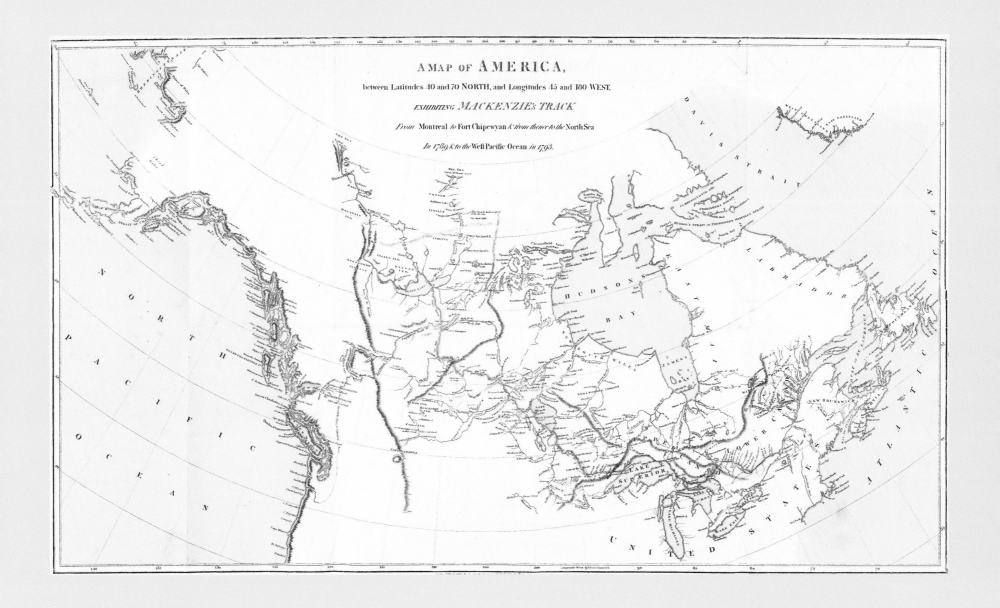

A MAP OF AMERICA,

between Latitudes 40 and 70 NORTH, and Longitudes 45 and 180 WEST.

EXHIBITING MACKENZIE'S TRACK

From Montreal *to* Fort Chipewyan & *from thence to the* North Sea

In 1789, & *to the* West Pacific Ocean *in* 1793.

Andrew Ellicott.

"Map of the Mississippi River."
In *The Journal of Andrew Ellicott*. Philadelphia, 1803.

Andrew Ellicott (1754-1820) was born in Pennsylvania and reared in Ellicott Mills, Maryland, a town founded by his father. The foremost surveyor of his day, Andrew Ellicott conducted numerous surveys to establish state and territorial boundaries, including the boundary between the United States and the Spanish possessions in Florida. He also surveyed the site of the nation's new capital at Washington, D.C. Ellicott elevated American surveying and cartography to a new level of precision and accuracy.

The Journal of Andrew Ellicott, late commissioner on behalf of the United States (Philadelphia, 1803) includes a map of the mouth of the Mississippi River, two maps of the Mississippi below the mouth of the Ohio River, and two maps of the Ohio. In addition, Ellicott mapped the upper Mississippi River to the Great Lakes and located the position of the mouth of the Missouri River quite accurately. An appendix to the *Journal* provides measurements, astronomical observations, and detailed calculations from his surveys in Florida and along the Mississippi River. Published at the time of the Louisiana Purchase, the *Journal* is also noteworthy because Ellicott advocates the acquisition of Louisiana by the United States as a way to keep the western states in the Union.

When Secretary of the Treasury Albert Gallatin commissioned Nicholas King to produce a new map of North America for the Lewis and Clark Expedition, he instructed King to incorporate Ellicott's work on the Mississippi River. When planning the expedition to the West, Thomas Jefferson turned to Ellicott for advice. Jefferson knew that no other American could match Ellicott's experience in making astronomical and field observations under trying conditions. Ellicott supplied Jefferson with a list of equipment that he thought should be taken on the expedition. He also instructed Meriwether Lewis in the use of the sextant and octant, regulated Lewis's chronometer, and devised a new type of artificial horizon for making field observations on the expedition.

(The Tracy W. McGregor Library of American History, Special Collections, University of Virginia Library)

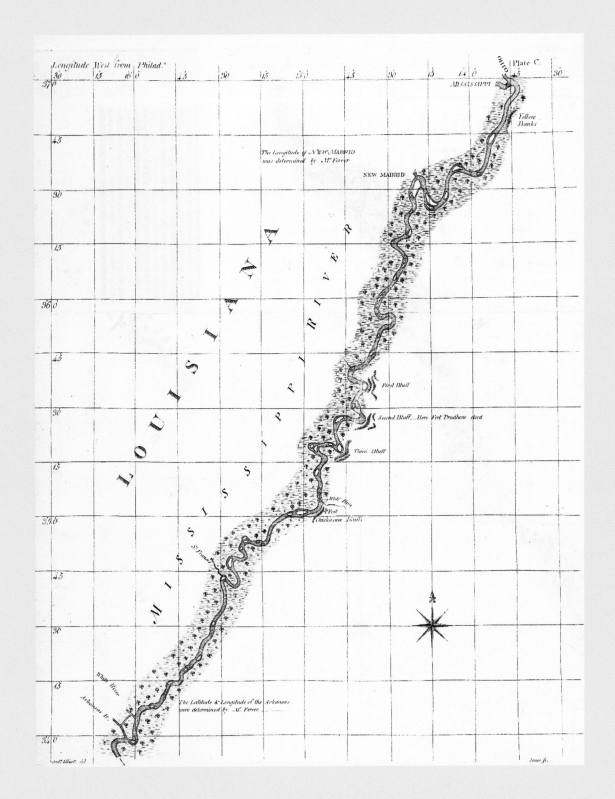

Longitude West from Philad.

Plate C.

Ohio

MISSISSIPPI

Yellow
Banks

The Longitude of NEW MADRID
was determined by Mr Ferrer

NEW MADRID

L O U I S I A N A

M I S S I S S I P P I R I V E R

First Bluff

Second Bluff....Here Fort Prudhome stood

Third Bluff

Wolf River

N Fort

Chickasaw Bluffs

St Francis

M I S S I S S I P P I

White River

Arkansas R.

The Latitude & Longitude of the Arkansas
were determined by Mr Ferrer.

Andw Ellicott del

Jones fe.

David Thompson.

"A map showing the Great Bend of the Missouri." 1798.

London-born David Thompson (1770-1857) began an apprenticeship at the age of fourteen as a clerk in the Hudson's Bay Company's Canadian offices. A few years later, Thompson learned surveying and astronomy from Philip Turnor, a compiler of the *Nautical Almanac*. In his capacity as Inland Surveyor for the Hudson's Bay Company, Turnor mapped a large portion of the shoreline of the Hudson Bay and several western rivers. Thompson was to have gone on Turnor's 1790 expedition to determine the exact location of and best route to Lake Athabasca, but a leg injury precluded his participation. Peter Fidler, who later succeeded Turnor as Inland Surveyor, took Thompson's place on the mission.

Thompson continued to work as a surveyor for the Hudson's Bay Company until 1797, when he left to join the North West Company. In 1811, Thompson became the first European to descend the length of the Columbia River. With Peter Fidler, he surveyed and mapped 16,000 miles of waterways in western Canada and the northwestern United States. Beginning in 1816, Thompson headed a ten-year commission to survey the border between Canada and the United States. Although he was one of the outstanding geographers of his day, he received little recognition during his lifetime. The narrative of his discoveries was not published until 1916.

In 1797-1798, Thompson surveyed and mapped the North West Company's trade route from Lake Superior to Lake Winnipeg. He returned to Lake Superior via the Assiniboine River, the Mandan villages, the Red River, and the headwaters of the Mississippi. During this odyssey Thompson discovered Turtle Lake, which is one of the sources of the Mississippi River, and he accurately determined the latitude and longitude of the Great Bend of the Missouri River near the Mandan villages.

Thompson's map proved to be an important resource for the Lewis and Clark Expedition. Following Albert Gallatin's instructions, Nicholas King incorporated Thompson's representation of the upper portion of the Missouri into the new map he prepared for the expedition (page 81). Meriwether Lewis may have traced Thompson's map of the Great Bend of the Missouri from materials in the possession of Edward Thornton, the British chargé d'affaires in Washington. Lewis and Clark carried this tracing on their journey to the Pacific Ocean.

The tracing pictured here is in the Geography and Map Division of the Library of Congress. A notation on the front of the map in Jefferson's hand reads: "Bend of the Missouri, Long. 101° 25' Lat. 47° 32' by Mr. Thomson astronomer to the N.W. Company in 1798." Another notation on the back of the tracing reads: "A sketch of the North Bend of the Missouri. This belongs to Capn. Lewis."

(Geography and Map Division of the Library of Congress)

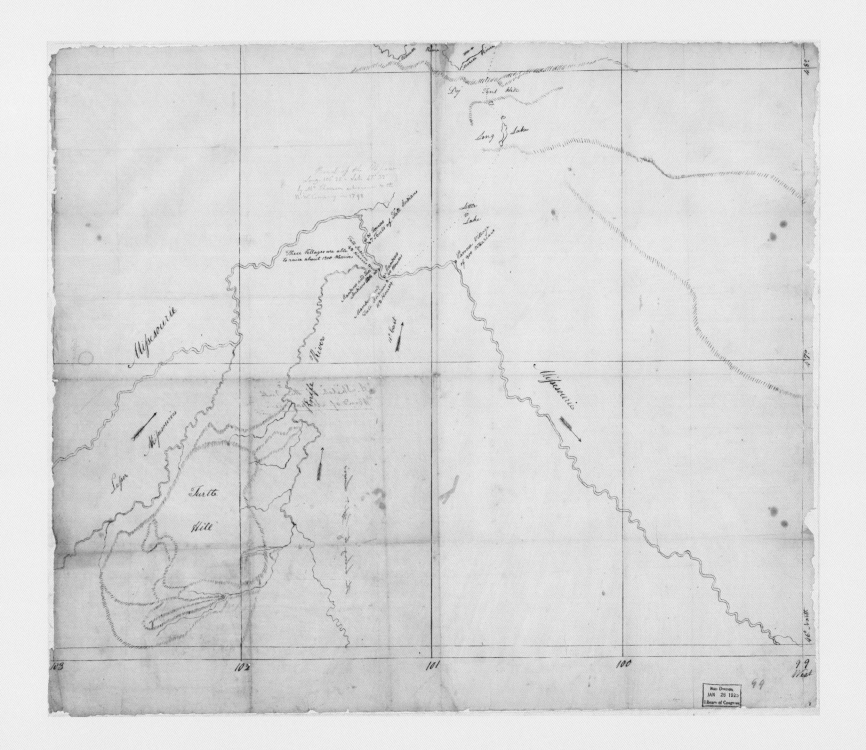

Aaron Arrowsmith.

"A Map Exhibiting all the New Discoveries in the Interior
Parts of North America." 1795, with additions to 1811.

Aaron Arrowsmith (1750-1823) began his career as a surveyor in England. He made several maps that appeared in John Cary's popular *Traveller's Companion*, an atlas of turnpike roads in England and Wales. In 1790 Arrowsmith started his own mapmaking firm. His maps and atlases soon earned him an international reputation for accuracy and fine engraving.

Arrowsmith produced his first map of North America in 1795 from the journals and surveys of western Canada held in the London archives of the Hudson's Bay Company. Arrowsmith's 1795 map (not shown) incorporates details from the surveys of Peter Fidler in the Northwest through 1792, Samuel Hearne's explorations west of the Hudson Bay, Alexander Mackenzie's journey to the Arctic Ocean in 1789, and George Vancouver's chart of the Northwest coast and the "River Oregan" (lower Columbia River, see page 71). The 1795 map shows a vestige of the "Great River of the West" and the Missouri River appears as a river fragment unconnected to either the "Stony Mountains" or the Mississippi River. Arrowsmith also includes a note stating that the "Stony Mountains" are "3520 Feet High above the Level of their Base and according to the Indian account is five Ridges in some parts."

The 1802 revision of the map of North America, shown here, delineates the complete length of the Missouri River as well as Mackenzie's journey to the Pacific in 1793. The depiction of the Missouri headwaters, which Arrowsmith studied from Peter Fidler's drawing of a map by the Blackfoot Indian Ac Ko Mo Ki, shows several streams joining into two branches of the Missouri that flow almost due east. The southern branch of the Missouri appears to be the main branch of the river and connects to the Knife River; the northern branch is a good representation of the actual course of the Missouri.

Although the revised map still shows a single ridge of mountains in the west, a note placed near the southern sources of the Missouri states: "Hereabout the Mountains divide into several low Ridges." This note, which was based on the reports of Fidler, Mackenzie, and Thompson, was more encouraging to Jefferson and Lewis than the note about the Stony Mountains on the 1795 map, which, unfortunately, turned out to be more accurate. Arrowsmith's map situates the Great Lake River on the western slopes of the mountain range and connects this river to the Columbia River with a dotted line. Since another note claims that this river can be descended to the sea in eight days, the Arrowsmith map supported the erroneous belief in a convenient route to the Pacific Ocean.

Nicholas King consulted both the 1795 and 1802 versions of Arrowsmith's map as he prepared his map for the Lewis and Clark Expedition (page 81). Lewis and Clark, in fact, carried the 1802 Arrowsmith map along on their journey. Thomas Jefferson owned the 1802 map as well as an 1802 edition of Arrowsmith's map of the United States. Arrowsmith's 1802 map of North America was certainly the most comprehensive map of the West available in 1802 and it was probably the most important map used in the planning of the Lewis and Clark Expedition.

The map shown here is the lower half of "A Map Exhibiting all the New Discoveries" from an edition labeled "1795, with additions to 1811." The lower half of the map is identical to the 1802 edition.

(The Tracy W. McGregor Library of American History, Special Collections, University of Virginia Library)

Nicholas King.

"Map of the Western part of North America." 1803.

Nicholas King (1771-1812) was born in England and raised in a family of surveyors and cartographers. He came to the United States in 1794 and worked as a surveyor in Philadelphia. In 1796 and 1797 he served as the first surveyor of Washington, D.C., an office he again held from 1803 until his death in 1812. King prepared maps related to the expeditions of Lewis and Clark, William Dunbar, Zebulon Pike, and others.

In March 1803, U.S. Secretary of the Treasury Albert Gallatin (1761-1849) asked King to prepare a comprehensive new map of western North America for the Lewis and Clark Expedition. Gallatin, who shared Jefferson's lifelong enthusiasm for science, geography, and the Indian cultures of North and Central America, played an active role in planning the expedition. He instructed King to incorporate the work of Ellicott, Cook, Vancouver, Arrowsmith, Mackenzie, Thompson, Mitchell, d'Anville, and Delisle into his map.

Although it copies liberally from the western portion of Aaron Arrowsmith's 1802 map of North America (page 79), the King map synthesizes the most advanced representations of the Missouri River system, including its relationship to the Pacific Northwest. King, in contrast to Arrowsmith, shows the northern branch of the Missouri as the main branch of the river and represents the northernmost source of the Missouri closer to the Great Lake River on the western slopes. The King map also differs from Arrowsmith's in that it depicts the Rocky Mountains not as a long, solid chain of mountains but as a shorter range that ends near the 45th parallel in today's Montana. Gaps in the range near the present-day Canadian border suggest the possibility of an easy crossing of the Continental Divide. King's map also tracks a southern branch of the Columbia skirting the southern end

of the Rockies. These latter concepts were probably based on the work of Fidler, Mackenzie, and Thompson. In addition, King's map affirms the pyramidal height-of-land theory by situating the source of the Rio Grande on a high plateau near the source of the Columbia River.

The actual Nicholas King map that Lewis and Clark carried on their expedition to the Pacific is in the Geography and Map Division of the Library of Congress.

(Geography and Map Division of the Library of Congress)

William Clark.

"A Map of part of the Continent of North America." 1810.

William Clark (1770-1838), whose family resided for a time near Charlottesville, grew up in Virginia and Kentucky. Although he received little formal education, he mastered frontier skills and the art of surveying. He followed in the footsteps of his older brother, George Rogers Clark, the great hero of the Revolutionary War, by joining the army and serving a command on the Mississippi River. William Clark was Meriwether Lewis's commanding officer in 1795-1796 and he and Lewis became friends. They remained friends after Clark resigned his army commission. While Lewis was serving as President Jefferson's personal secretary, Clark visited him and also met Jefferson.

The three men doubtlessly discussed Jefferson's dream of finding a route to the Pacific Ocean. After Jefferson selected Lewis to lead the expedition to the Pacific, Clark eagerly accepted Lewis's offer to share the command. As Jefferson wrote to a government official, "William Clarke accepts with great glee the office of going with Capt. Lewis up the Missouri." Following the expedition, Clark served as superintendent of Indian Affairs and then governor of the Missouri Territory.

In preparation for the expedition to the Pacific, William Clark trained himself to be an able cartographer. During the winter of 1803-1804 Clark studied the maps and geographic information that Lewis brought to Camp Dubois near St. Louis. He also practiced using the sextant and the octant. William Clark was a fast learner, perhaps due to his surveying experience. Before the Corps of Discovery left the St. Louis area, Clark produced a map of part of upper Louisiana and a table of distances to the Pacific coast. By the spring of 1805, when the expedition team had advanced as far as Fort Mandan (in Washburn, North Dakota), Clark had produced the route maps of the Missouri River from St. Louis and a general map of the Missouri River system and the Northwest.

Twenty-eight arduous months after setting off, the Lewis and Clark Expedition returned to a triumphant welcome in St. Louis on September 23, 1806. Upon hearing news of the success of the expedition, Jefferson wrote of his "unspeakable joy." As Lewis and Clark hurried on to Washington, Clark brought along an updated map of the West that he had prepared the previous winter at Fort Clatsop (Oregon) on the Pacific coast. Nicholas King copied both the Fort Mandan map and the updated map made at Fort Clatsop.

Over the next few years Clark continued to update his map, producing in 1810 the version shown here. This map includes information gathered from the 1807-1808 explorations of the Yellowstone basin by Corps of Discovery members George Drouillard and John Colter. Clark's 1810 map also incorporates the findings from Zebulon Pike's expeditions to the southern Rockies and upper Mississippi River; James Wilkinson's expedition on the Arkansas River; William Dunbar's explorations of the Ouachita River; and Thomas Freeman's journey to the Red River.

William Clark's map surpasses its predecessors by presenting a radically new and remarkably accurate view of the upper Missouri and its connections with the Columbia River basin. The map is also notable for its representation of the western mountains as multiple ranges rather than a single strand of mountains. This advance in geographical knowledge finally extinguished the idea of a Northwest Passage to India via the Missouri River and marked the end of the long-cherished hope of finding a short portage to the Pacific.

Clark's original map is in the William Robertson Coe Collection of Western Americana, Beinecke Rare Book and Manuscript Library, Yale University.

(William Robertson Coe Collection of Western Americana, Beinecke Rare Book and Manuscript Library, Yale University)

A MAP
of part of the Continent of
North America

"A Map of Lewis and Clark's Track."

In *History of the Expedition under the Command of Captains Lewis and Clark, to the Sources of the Missouri, Thence across the Rocky Mountains and down the River Columbia to the Pacific Ocean. Performed during the years 1804-5-6 . . . .* Paul Allen, editor. Philadelphia, 1814.

Meriwether Lewis (1774-1809) was born in Albemarle County, Virginia. His name reflects the union of two families—the Meriwethers and the Lewises—who were early settlers and large landholders in the Albemarle area. After a short spell in northeast Georgia, Meriwether Lewis returned to Albemarle County in 1789 to further his education. He tried farming briefly before entering the military and rising to the rank of captain. In 1801 he became Thomas Jefferson's personal secretary. Two years later, Jefferson chose him to lead the expedition to the Pacific Ocean. After returning from the expedition, Lewis was appointed governor of the upper Louisiana Territory, a post he held until his death in 1809.

Thomas Jefferson's instructions for the Lewis and Clark Expedition reveal that he expected the expeditionary team to gather a wealth of scientific and geographic data. Jefferson requested that copies of the expedition notes and observations be "put into the care of your most trust-worthy of your attendants." Lewis sent Jefferson a letter from Fort Mandan in the spring of 1805 affirming that "We have encouraged our men to keep journals, and seven of them do so." Lewis, himself, was responsible for recording most of the scientific findings of the expedition, including observations on flora, fauna, minerals, Indian languages, and celestial and geographic conditions. William Clark, meanwhile, concentrated on charting the expeditionary route, preparing maps, and logging each day's events.

After the completion of the expedition, Jefferson expected Lewis to turn the raw notes and data he had amassed on the expedition into a finished "scientific" account. Lewis had made only limited progress on this project at the time of his death in 1809. The completion of the work fell to William Clark. Clark arranged for Nicholas Biddle, a respected scholar and writer in Philadelphia, to prepare the official journals of the expedition for publication. Biddle eventually hired Paul Allen to complete the editing. In 1814 Allen issued a two-volume set of the journals, *History of the Expedition under the Command of Captains Lewis and Clark*. The published journals included "A Map of Lewis and Clark's Track, Across the Western Portion of North America From the Mississippi to the Pacific Ocean," a version of Clark's 1810 map.

(The Tracy W. McGregor Library of American History, Special Collections, University of Virginia Library)

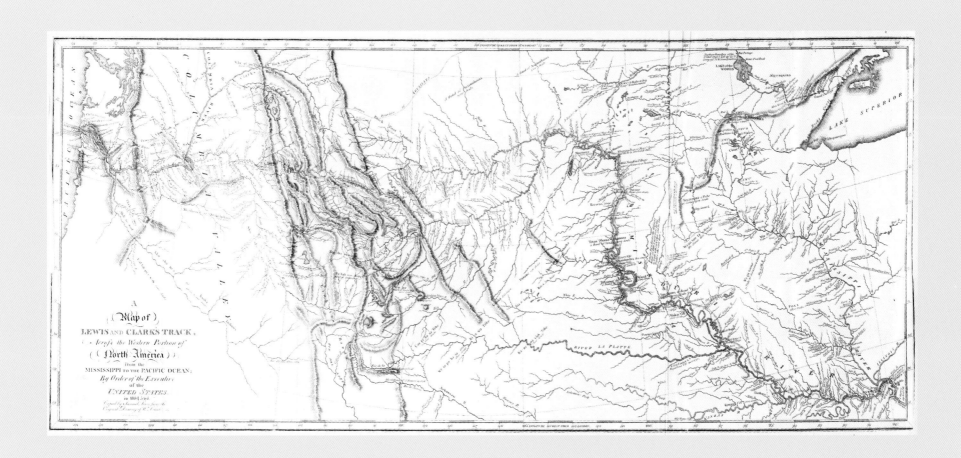

A Map of LEWIS AND CLARKS TRACK, Across the Western Portion of North America, From the MISSISSIPPI to the PACIFIC OCEAN; By Order of the Executive of the UNITED STATES, in 1804.5.&6.

This book was made possible by the generosity of

Mr. and Mrs. Peter A. Agelasto III
Mr. and Mrs. Richard E. Ailstock
Mr. and Mrs. Philip H. Anns
Mr. and Mrs. William F. Muenster
Mr. and Mrs. Lloyd T. Smith, Jr.
University of Virginia Lewis and Clark Bicentennial Project
The Watterson Foundation